SOUTH YORKSHIRE
FOLK
TALES

T0341941

SOUTH YORKSHIRE
FOLK TALES

SIMON HEYWOOD

WITH DAMIEN BARKER

The
History
Press

SH

For Shonaleigh and Isaac

I've told my tale,
Thee tell thine.

***

DB

In memory of Roy and Reg

Wordsmiths, fibbers, allotment enthusiasts,
and keepers of forgotten lore.
May these words prompt many questions
from the grandchildren you never met.

First published 2015

The History Press
97 St George's Place,
Cheltenham, Gloucestershire, GL50 3QB
www.thehistorypress.co.uk

Reprinted 2016, 2020

British Library Cataloguing in Publication Data.
A catalogue record for this book is available from the British Library.

ISBN 978 0 7509 6164 6

Typesetting and origination by The History Press
Printed in Great Britain by TJ International Ltd, Padstow, Cornwall

When the legends die, the dreams end;
there is no more greatness.

Attributed to Tecumseh (1768–1813),
Shawnee chief

CONTENTS

MAP OF SOUTH YORKSHIRE (NOT TO SCALE)

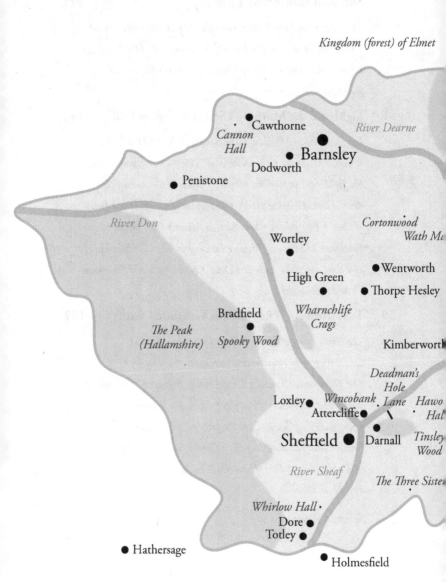

● Wentbridge

Barnsdale Bar

Robin Hood's Well

River Don

*Great North Road
(Ermine Street)*

Barnsdale Forest

● Thorne

● Hatfield

Hickleton
●

Lindholme·

Hatfield Chase

Barnburgh
●

/ *Hangman
Stone Road*

● **Doncaster**

● Rossington

Swinton
●

Conisbrough
●

● Kilnhurst

Rawmarsh   ● Hooton Roberts

● Thrybergh

Rotherham

Tickhill ●

● Whiston   ● Wickersley

Roche Abbey

+

Aston
● ●

● Firbeck

wallownest   Laughton-en-le-Morthen

River Rother

Wales
●

● Kiveton Park

INTRODUCTION

In June 2012, the Sheffield band Reverend and the Makers appeared live on BBC *Breakfast Time*, to promote a new release. The presenter, Bill Turnbull, was curious about this successful band's reluctance to relocate to London. What was it about their Sheffield home, he asked frontman Jon McClure, that made it so special?

McClure did not hesitate.

'Understatement,' he replied firmly.

Understatement seems to run deep in South Yorkshire. For much of its history, the place hardly existed – in official terms. An old name, *Hallamshire*, refers to a loosely defined area on the right bank of the River Don, but the southern reaches of Yorkshire were always part of its West Riding. The county of South Yorkshire, comprising the metropolitan boroughs of Barnsley, Doncaster, Sheffield and Rotherham, was created in 1974. It now appears as a historic centre of mining, metalworking and other industries, garlanded by legend-rich beauty spots, including the Peak District, the Yorkshire Dales, the Vale of York, the North York Moors, and Sherwood Forest, which can seem to outshine its own wealth of landscape, tradition and history. The understatement, however, is deceptive.

Traffic along eastern Britain has always had to skirt round the head of the Humber, fording or bridging its tributaries. The landscape drained by these smaller rivers – including the Don, Dearne, Sheaf, and Rother – forms a natural barrier to north–south traffic.

It is therefore no coincidence that local historians[1] have long recognised the area now known as South Yorkshire as a frontier zone. Nor is it chance that the frontier has lasted longer than any of the territories and peoples it has divided. It has separated prehistoric tribe from prehistoric tribe; Celt from Roman; province from province, in Roman Britain; Dark-Age Briton from Dark-Age Saxon; and medieval English from conquering Vikings. Today, the same boundary divides the northern English county of Yorkshire from the counties of the English Midlands.

This durable frontier has, in turn, left its own marks on the landscapes that defined it. The name of the village suburb of Dore means, as it sounds, a door, or threshold. According to the great nineteenth-century folklorist Sidney Addy, the River Sheaf, which gives Sheffield its name, bears a name that similarly means boundary. The Red Lion Inn at Gleadless is still said to straddle the county line, and the stream that marked the county boundary, the Shirebrook, ran through the pub's cellar. Legend reports that late drinkers in modern times would cross the room to avail themselves of Derbyshire's more liberal licensing hours.[2]

But, paradoxically, the main thoroughfare of eastern Britain has always run right through the area. Over the centuries, the main route seems to have oscillated, like a gigantic plucked bowstring, up and down the Don Valley: from the Ermine or Icknield Streets that the Romans paved, to the Great North Road (now the A1) that Robin Hood watched, and back today to the route of the M1.

So South Yorkshire has always been – so to speak – less ancient boundary than ancient checkpoint. Such places tend to be fought over. Sheffield's history began with Celtic and Roman fortresses, overlooking the lower Don river crossings. In 1966 archaeologists announced that earthworks at Butcher's Orchard, North Anston,

---

1   'The district ... has no historical unity, except that it is, and always has been, emphatically a *border* district' (Armitage 1897: 1). The odd-seeming name of one South Yorkshire village, *Wales*, testifies (again, more or less as it sounds) to the persistence of British communities within Anglo-Saxon South Yorkshire.

2   'The Red Lion', www.pub-explorer.com/syorks/pub/redlioninnsheffield.htm, accessed 15-4-2014.

were, in fact, the remains of a medieval house, or maybe some seventeenth-century fishponds. There was disappointment in the local community at this announcement, because the earthworks had long been regarded as marks of an ancient battlefield.[3] In context, this was a fairly reasonable supposition.

The terrain is hilly towards the west and flatter towards the east. Heath, woodland and wetland form its natural cover. Sheffield, indeed, remains one of the leafiest cities in Europe. The region's first prehistoric farmers largely kept to the uplands; later, when the wildwoods were cleared, the plough conquered the valleys. But throughout the Middle Ages there remained a great deal of managed hunting reserve: that is, *forest*, in the original sense of the word – outdoor playgrounds for the rich, sometimes, but not always, thickly wooded. We read that Barnsdale, Robin Hood's favoured haunt, was not a forest in this sense, but was instead a remote tract of waste woodland. Sherwood, by contrast, was, legally, a forest. It existed as such by 1130 (Mitchell 1970: 16). There were many other forests and chases nearby, partly because local princes and great landowning families dominated the area's early history. Then came the medieval church, and the great landowning abbeys of Roche and Beauchief.

But when these great abbeys were ruins, South Yorkshire's rivers began to lend water-power to the knife-grinding and metalworking trades, and the area's centre of gravity shifted westward back towards them, from the medieval towns of Conisbrough and Doncaster to the well-watered hills. From the seventeenth to the early nineteenth centuries, Sheffield's Cutlers' Company came to preside over a self-reliant, well-organised, confident and cohesive working community, whose backbone was the independent craftsmen, or little mesters, whose tradition of workmanship has lasted till the present day – just about. Thereafter, industrial production in the area was destined to be organised on an even larger scale. Wood- and then coal-burning industry created substantial working and middle classes. Later,

---

3   *Morning Telegraph*, 11-6-1966 (RALS).

℘

trade unionism inherited the area's old instinct for social cohesion and tight community. Other expressions of the same instinct, meanwhile, took many forms. In the earlier 1800s, in most English cities, blind street musicians were buskers or beggars, but in Sheffield they were an organised and prosperous guild, a central pillar of the rapidly burgeoning urban community. The sinking of pits and the spread of pit villages across the coalfields – a recent process, not complete until well into the twentieth century – sealed modern South Yorkshire's character as an industrial centre. The county's central place in the modern labour movement – lately expressed in an unofficial and affectionate title, the People's Republic of South Yorkshire – was therefore grounded in old community traditions.

Well indeed were those old traditions called *radical*. Sheffield town stood with Parliament in the Civil War. When Royalists dug themselves in at Sheffield Castle, the castle was captured and razed. Little trace of it now remains above ground. In the 1790s, Sheffield would throw a street party, and roast an ox to divide among the city poor, whenever the revolutionary French armies won a battle (Mather 1862: xx). In the Yorkshire coalfields, the miners' old enemy, Winston Churchill, was never quite accepted as the irreproachable figure he is often presumed to be elsewhere.[4] In more recent times, community activism saved a Sheffield suburb, Walkley, from demolition, and also stopped the construction of an inner-city bypass through the suburb of Heeley; Heeley City Farm was created instead. Most spectacularly, there were the miners' strikes, culminating in the great strike of 1984–85. The coalfields celebrated unabashedly when Margaret Thatcher died in 2013. It is easy to feel that Robin Hood of Barnsdale would have done likewise.

---

4   The poet Ian MacMillan, from Darfield: 'My mam and dad … venerated Churchill; … Round our way, of course, he was remembered for other things as well, like the authorising of the use of troops during a strike.' www.yorkshirepost.co.uk/news/debate/columnists/ian-mcmillan-tomorrow-i-will-mourn-what-we-have-lost-continuity-collectivism-and-pride-1-5587149, accessed 4-9-2013.

The region's storytelling traditions bear witness to all these currents and conditions. The earliest stories of South Yorkshire were recorded mainly by the educated and powerful; they tell of warlike kings and miraculous monks, as one might expect. Tales of knights, saints and marvels endure today in villages like Barnburgh and Hickleton. Radical Sheffield added more recent ghosts to the mix, like Old Moult of Wickersley Grange. Tales abound still of the exploits of striking miners against the police, or highwaymen against the judge, or forest outlaws against the sheriff; and stories of ghosts and portents haunted the pits until the end – just as they haunt the notorious accident blackspot at Stocksbridge bypass to this day, in the shadow of the steelworks.

The more recent material is naturally more plentiful. Some of it was recorded by interested scholars and educated people, from Abraham de la Pryme in the seventeenth-century to Sidney Addy in the nineteenth, or David Clarke in the present day. Radical and Victorian Sheffield saw a flowering of local and topical literature, with writers and poets including Joseph Mather, Ebenezer Elliott, Joseph Woolhouse, and Sidney Addy; other tales were written by local historians researching their own communities, such as John Chessman, Cyril Wilson, and Charles Colley Bailey. An increasing wealth of older, out-of-copyright material is now freely available online – work by local writers such as C.J. Davison Ingledew and John Tomlinson for instance. Rotherham Archives and Local Studies also stocks a wealth of newspapers and news sources and will be noted in sources as RALS. Of increasing value, too, as primary sources, are blogs and social media sites such as the Sheffield Forum and Sheffield History. In some cases we have had the privilege of collecting stories by word of mouth or personal correspondence. Sadly, but inevitably, we have not always been able to give due credit to all of the original storytellers, but we have never lost sight of the fact that this book is little more than a homage to their often understated expertise.

The collection that follows is, of course, necessarily selective. The traditional tales of South Yorkshire include some long tales; but many are short. Such snippets of story have a label in academic jargon: they are 'dites', or sayings – a 'dite' being 'a statement that implies but does not recount a narrative' (McCormick and White 2011). The landscapes of South Yorkshire, both ancient and modern, are saturated with such sayings. We might, indeed, call them narrative understatements.

With regret, nevertheless, we have had to set aside many of South Yorkshire's notable characters and reported spectres and apparitions. We have done this partly for considerations of space, but sometimes because we were simply unable to find out enough about them. We have not found enough to say about King Harold Godwinson, said to have lived at Kiveton Park;[5] or Martha Hatfield, the eleven-year-old Wise Virgin of Laughton-en-le-Morthen;[6] or the Indian prince said to haunt Scholes Lane, between Thorpe Hesley and Greasbrough;[7] or 'Lindum Hall … where there was a barn full of white sparrows,' besides other 'giants and queer characters' whose tales were told in the West Riding even before 'those collier chaps … started calling it South Yorkshire';[8] or the poet Thomas Gray, who, some say, composed his famous *Elegy* at Aston;[9] or Dance David, the hermit of the Delfs in Hill Top.[10] Neither have we had much to say about South Yorkshire's wealth of traditions beyond its stories: its calendar customs, well dressings, mischief nights, or seasonal ceremonial plays and customs such as the Harthill Tup.[11]

We were similarly unable to make enough of a story about the ghosts of Monks Bretton Priory or Carbrook Hall; or the still-restless ghost of the sailor who survived all the perils of the sea, only to drown, with terrible irony, in the basement of the Ship Inn at Shalesmoor in the great Sheffield Flood of 1864; the Crying Boy,

5 See the letter by Charles Colley Bailey to *Rotherham Advertiser*, 22-7-1988 (RALS).

6 *Dinnington and Maltby Guardian*, 21-9-2006 (RALS).

7 *Rotherham Advertiser*, 6-12-1952, 20-12-1952 (RALS).

8 Kitchen, *Brother to the Ox*, 1981 (1939).

9 *The Star*, 2-6-1959; *Morning Telegraph*, 4-4-1972 (RALS).

10 Sanderson, *A Layman's Look at the History, People and Places of Oughtibridge, Worrall, and Wharncliffe Side* (1999)

11 Derek Leigh, in *Harthill Parish Magazine*, December 1979 (RALS).

Carbrook Hall, Attercliffe

a supposedly cursed painting that was rumoured to start house fires in the houses where it was displayed (actually based on reports of a house fire in Rotherham in 1985, with the idea of a curse added by tabloid journalists in a successful attempt to add spice and interest to the story); or most of the many White and Grey and Green Ladies which abound in the county, as they do elsewhere; or the numerous mysterious sightings of UFOs, big cats, and other instances of the strange and paranormal in contemporary life. Armed police were called out to a sighting of a big cat near Rotherham in 1997;[12] nor was this the first local sighting of a 'massive black cat' or 'jet black creature with staring yellow eyes'.[13] We have also left aside most rumours of tunnels, caves, and secret passages, which cling to sites such as Kirkstead Abbey Grange, Monks Bretton, Roche Abbey and Sheffield Manor – even though these rumours sometimes seem equally well founded. Cave systems were discovered under Maltby by workmen at Herne Hill

12   *Rotherham Advertiser*, 2-5-1997, 6-6-1997; *Dinnington and Maltby Guardian*, 30-5-1997 (RALS).

13   *Rotherham Star*, 14-1-1994; *Yorkshire Post*, 15-1-1994 (RALS).

in 1973,[14] and tunnels by a twelve-year-old boy at Roche Abbey in 1977.[15] Sheffield is said to be honeycombed with tunnels, particularly those which once connected Sheffield Manor with Sheffield Castle, in the time of the imprisonment of Mary Stuart, Queen of Scots, at Sheffield; as elsewhere in the county, these rumours are sometimes shown to be (so to speak) not without foundation.[16] The part that tunnels (or rumours of tunnels) play in local legend is shown in one example we have given in full, that of Haworth Hall, although tunnels have also been mentioned in the case of Jasper the Whistler (see Chapter 8). Last but not least, we certainly wish we could have found more to say about Kilnhurst's 1881 shower of frogs.[17] The one report we have been able to find consists, in its entirety, of the following two sentences:

> A shower of frogs fell on Kilnhurst Railway Station during a thunderstorm. Officials took some time to clear them all off the platform.

Now that – one might say – is understatement.

We have also left out some stories, including well-known cases like Springheeled Jack, and the Stocksbridge Bypass hauntings, purely because they have already been recorded by other writers, such as David Clarke, Liz Linahan, and Jenny Randles. Finally – and also with regret – we have not considered the storytelling traditions of the post-war immigrant communities to the region's urban centres. We know from personal experience that the name of Anansi, the Afro-Caribbean spider-trickster, is remembered on the streets of Pitsmoor in Sheffield. Perhaps Akbar, or Birbal, or Pan Twardowski,[18] or other heroes of world folklore, have joined the Kilkenny Devil

---

14 *Rotherham Star*, 10-12-1980; *Rotherham Advertiser*, 23-6-1978, 27-3-1981 (RALS).

15 *Morning Telegraph*, 28-5-1977 (RALS).

16 'Interesting Discovery of a Subterranean Passage in Sheffield', *Sheffield Independent*, 20-5-1896 (Sheffield Archives and Local Studies).

17 'Looking Back: 100 Years Ago', *Rotherham Advertiser*, 6-8-1981 (RALS).

18 SH is grateful to Grace Suszek for knowledge of this legendary Polish sorcerer and trafficker with the Devil.

The Cholera Monument, Sheffield

and the witch of Semerwater among the many bequests of immigrants to South Yorkshire's storytelling. We hope so.

In this region of well dressing, interest in wells and witchcraft has remained lively. Sidney Addy, in the late nineteenth century, recorded that children were afraid to fetch water from the Sparken Well at Dore, because it was inhabited by a spirit. Another well by Roche Abbey had, he said, the reputation of granting wishes. At Jordanthorpe – now a council estate – there grew a rowan or 'wiggin' tree that had been planted 'to keep the witches out of the churn' – spoiled butter being commonly blamed on witchcraft in South Yorkshire and beyond, and rowan being an equally common charm against witchcraft. Belief in witches is evidenced in the county. Joan Jurdie of Rossington was twice investigated for witchcraft by the Mayor of Doncaster in 1605.[19] The Jordanthorpe wiggin tree blew down in a gale in 1891, but almost a century later, Anston Town Well was restored, with 'people still showing interest in drinking the water from the wells' and samples of the well-water being recommended for analysis by local councillors.[20] In the 1970s, some Anston residents had used the wells all their life.[21] In 1976, a nineteenth-century well was rediscovered at Whiston and was remembered by the locals for its 'definite aphrodisiac qualities' as well as its efficacy against coughs and sneezes.[22] In the same year, the *Rotherham Star* reported that a tenant had refused a council house on the grounds that it was haunted, and a council employee informed journalists that the complaint was not unique.[23]

Finally, it is pleasingly necessary to note that South Yorkshire has also been a major centre for folk tale research, from the early antiquarians John Harrison and Abraham de la Pryme, to Joseph Hunter (1783–1861) and Sidney Oldall Addy (1848–1933). Our sources of inspiration also include Professor John Widdowson, founder-director of the National Centre for English Cultural Tradition at Sheffield University and the Centre for English Traditional Heritage; Dr David Clarke, now of Sheffield Hallam University; and many others. We would like to extend a particular thanks to all those others who shared their stories and knowledge of South Yorkshire with us, and commented on early drafts, especially Catherine Bannister; Chris Coates; Alice Collins; Paul and Liz Davenport; Susie Doncaster; Leila Dudley Edwards; Dave Eyre; Gordon Ferguson; Ilan Fertig; Bob and Chris Fitt; Helen Frances; Alan Griffith; Dane Holt; Chris Ingram; Peter Loades; Chris Nickson; Pete Sandford; Shonaleigh; Jim White; and Mike Wild; as well as Daniel Loades, whose photography inspired

19   Parkinson 1889: 150ff; Ewen 1933: 199ff; de la Pryme 1869: 288–89.

20   *Worksop Guardian*, 24-10-1986 (RALS).

21   *Rotherham Advertiser*, 30-6-1978 (RALS).

22   *Sheffield Star*, 24-9-1976 (RALS).

23   *Rotherham Star*, 4-6-1976 (RALS).

the illustrations. We are delighted to acknowledge the invaluable help and professionalism of Barnsley, Doncaster, Rotherham and Sheffield libraries. We are also indebted to colleagues in Creative Writing at the University of Derby, not only for introducing us to each other, but also for funding a period of research leave in autumn 2012. Finally, we would like to express our appreciation for our fellow-authors in The History Press's *Folk Tales* series, particularly Amy Douglas, Maureen James and David Phelps, for inspiration and example.

This is a verbal portrait of South Yorkshire's storytelling; it is not, so to speak, a verbal photograph of it. Where we felt the need to reshape fragmentary sources, to bring out what we hope is the tales' essential spirit, we have done so. At other times, we have told the stories as they were told to us, often word for word. Apart from some silent minor editing to keep punctuation consistent, it should be clear where we have done what. We have done our best to give full references for readers who want to consult our sources directly, and we welcome correspondence from those wishing to discuss these stories in more detail. We hope that our portrait has done justice to its subject by affording some entertainment to the real artists and keepers of these tales: the people of South Yorkshire. If we fail, it's our own fault.

Simon Heywood and Damien Barker
January 2015

1

BEGINNINGS

CARCONAN ON THE DON

Conisbrough Castle stands at the meeting place of two rivers, the Don and the Dearne. Old as the castle is, its foundations are older; there were other strongholds in the place before it.

The story of these strongholds ranges across many lands and generations, but it begins in the long dark years before Arthur ruled in Britain.

In those days, King Conan Meriadoc ruled in London. There were greedy and heartless men in plenty in Britain then – and

Conisbrough Castle

kings were worse than most – but Conan was the worst of them all. He was an evil man – cruel and small-minded. It was Conan who built the first fortress on the Don, because his family had ruled there time out of mind. He named it after himself: Carconan, the stronghold of Conan.

Cruel as he was, King Conan was the commander of all the legions of Roman Britain. He treated them as a private army. As king and commander, he answered only to the Roman emperor himself, and he knew that the emperor was weak. The Roman legionaries themselves, too, were more British than the Britons, having settled in the island many generations ago, in the long years of peace; they knew no king, and no commander, but Conan.

And, in these dark days, it was good that Britain had Conan and his legions. The island was ravaged day and night by Saxon brigands, pirates and savages from out of the dark north. They came by night in carved longships, marching inland, burning and plundering. King Conan and his private army were the only protection against them.

But one island was too small an empire for Conan, and no sooner had he built his new fortress at Carconan than he abandoned it, and left Britain altogether in search of conquest and plunder overseas. And he took the legions with him, leaving the island of Britain utterly defenceless. The Saxons fell on Britain like a wolf on the fold. Amid the havoc, the fortress of Carconan, newly built though it was, fell into ruin. Conan, meanwhile, was lucky in his plundering, and he carved himself out a whole new kingdom along the western coasts of Europe.

Then, at last, he told his victorious armies that they were legionaries no longer, but settlers and family men. The north-western coasts of Europe were now their home, and he would see to it that the British tongue would be spoken in the new kingdom forever. This was the sort of detail that Conan thought important; he was happy to abandon his homeland, but he was going to force those around him to speak his own mother tongue.

Conan's new colony now needed women and children, and so he remembered his island home again, and sent word, telling the lords of the Britons to send him unmarried women. He ordered new brides for his men by the shipload. They must speak British, he insisted, so that they could teach the British tongue to their children.

At this request, the Britons were aghast. Conan had already taken every able-bodied fighting man from the island. Now he wanted the women as well. It was as if he meant to make a desert of the island altogether. But still the Britons feared Conan's anger, and so the free women of Britain were sent off to Gaul. Many even went willingly, thinking it would be safer to follow King Conan than to stay in Britain and face the Saxons.

Most of the women never arrived. Their ships were wrecked in storms and lost on the lonely coasts. Many drowned. Saxon pirates fell on the rest, and took them as slaves. There are many stories of the sorrows of those days.

So, in the end, Conan never got his brides from Britain. He did not let this deter him though. He simply ordered his legionaries to take wives from the local people. The British soldiers went courting among the tribes of Gaul, and made marriage settlements with the local families, as the custom was. The Gaulish tribes were happy enough to make friendly treaties with these powerful incomers. Soon every legionary who wanted a wife had one from among the Gaulish women.

And then, once this was done, Conan ordered his men to cut the Gaulish women's tongues out. He did not want the Gaulish tongue spoken, he said, where the children of his new kingdom might hear it. He wanted them to grow up speaking British.

The thing was done. Conan's legionaries were obedient men, and they willingly handed their new wives over to their king's torturers. Some tore the women's tongues out with their own hands. The women themselves had no recourse or protection from this treatment. By Gaulish custom, they could not appeal to their own families; and, in any case, the Gaulish chieftains could hardly defy Conan. In the weeks and months which followed, a strange silence seemed to settle over the western coasts.

Perhaps as a result, Conan's new kingdom somehow got a strange new name. People began to call it the Half-Silent Realm.

And all this time, the old stronghold of Carconan on the Don still stood silent and derelict. But then a strange thing seemed to happen. People who lived on the banks of the rivers – people who knew nothing of Conan's adventures across the seas – began to fear the ruined fortress. Anyone who lingered nearby by night, so it was said, would hear women's voices echoing eerily, weeping and mourning in the empty ruin. There were strange words to be heard in these voices, words which could not be understood. The place got a bad name, and for many years nobody set foot in it at all.

The years passed. Conan prospered. He lived long, and died in his bed, and was buried in his new kingdom. In the years that followed, his descendants prospered, too. His children and grand-children ruled across the narrow seas as princes, still speaking the British tongue. In Britain, the Saxon plundering went on, and the island fell into a Dark Age.

In the midst of the darkness, a new king arose over the Britons: one even worse, in his way, than Conan had been.

The new king was Vortigern the Thin, a weak and greedy man. The Britons hated him. He could raise no army to protect himself, and so, rather than lose his throne to British rebels, Vortigern took the Saxon pirates themselves into his service, as mercenary soldiers. It was a shameful thing for a king to do, to pay the enemy himself for protection, but the Saxons and their royal client were well matched: they would have fought for anyone who paid, and Vortigern would have paid anyone to do his fighting for him.

The Saxon chieftain was called Hengest, and he had a brother called Horsa. Hengest was a shrewd and practical man. King Vortigern offered him gold and silver, but Hengest laughed.

'If you want me to fight for you, king, then offer me three gifts. Only three things. Such is the custom of my people. Give me a bull's hide; and the knife that slaughtered the bull and flayed it, with the blood still on it; and as much land as I can hide within it. A hide of land is what we call it. Promise me a hide of land, and I will fight for you.'

Vortigern certainly thought this a strange request, but it seemed to him that Hengest was a strange and savage man, so he scratched his head, and promised Hengest that he would have his bull's hide of land.

And on those terms, Vortigern and Hengest went to war against the British rebels. Hengest proved a master of war and a terror to his enemies, and when they returned to London, Vortigern was a king indeed, as great a king as any before Arthur; and all his enemies feared him.

When the wars were over, and the victory feast was in preparation, Vortigern remembered his promise to Hengest. He sent his bemused servants out to the paddock, to kill and flay the nearest bull, and to bring him the hide and the bloody knife. Then, before the whole court, when the feast was at its height, Vortigern presented Hengest with the hide and the bloody knife, and invited him to choose his land – and hide it in the bull's skin, as the Saxon saying put it.

And Hengest took the hide and the bloody knife, and with them he travelled the whole of Britain through, looking this way and that, until he came to the place where the Don meets the Dearne. There he lifted his eyes up, and looked for the first time on the haunted ruins of Carconan.

Hengest knew nothing of the strange stories that surrounded the place, and he liked the look of it. So, taking the bloody knife in one hand, and the hide in the other, he cut carefully at the hide, cutting it into a long spiral strip, as thin as a thread and many miles in length, like greasy gossamer. And then, one morning not long afterwards, some miles from the ruined fortress and with his warriors and followers watching, Hengest drove a wooden stake into the ground, and fastened one end of his leather thread to it.

Then Hengest set off walking. He paid out the thread as he went, pegging it out behind him, walking in a great curve mile after mile, all day until evening.

At evening he came back to the place he had started, and fastened both ends of the leather strip to the same post.

And everything within the long loop he claimed as his hide of land. It was a huge estate indeed, in fact a small kingdom: the whole valley of the Dearne and many miles beyond it. The Saxons cheered, and hailed Hengest as king, and Hengest's brother Horsa clapped him on the shoulder.

'You have hooked a big fish today, brother,' he said.

'Then the Hook-land is what I shall call it,' Hengest replied, and the land he had taken he called England, which is Hook-land in the Saxon tongue. It was the first place in Britain that was ever called England and the name stuck. Hengest made England a kingdom for himself, and a homeland for his Saxons, and he built himself a great wooden longhouse over the ruins of Carconan: a place where a chieftain could feast with his warriors and heroes, and hear old tales told. He called it Thancaster, the Stronghold of the Leather Band, and it was the second fortress built on the hill where the rivers meet.

At first, Thancaster seemed to prosper; the gleam of its lanterns and the echo of its talk and music spread far and wide each night, across the river valleys.

All was not well for Hengest, however. For the native British hated him as much as they hated Vortigern. By themselves they could do nothing against him, he was so strong, but across the narrow seas, King Conan's descendants – their distant fellow-countrymen – were still ruling the Half-Silent Realm. They still spoke the British tongue, after their own fashion, and when word crossed the narrow seas that their old family fortress, Carconan, had been torn down, rebuilt by a Saxon ruler, and given a strange new Saxon name, Conan's heirs swore revenge.

And then there was war. Two princes of the house of Conan crossed the narrow seas to Britain. Their names were Aurel and Uther, and by right of descent from their forefather Conan Meriadoc, they claimed the throne of London and the whole island of Britain. They came with a great army, and the native British flocked to the princes' banners to swell their ranks. There was a British lord, Eldol of the Dragon-Hill, who swore that he would lead Hengest by the nose like a pig to the slaughter, with his own hands, before the two princes.

Vortigern the Thin was swiftly overthrown. He fled, and was hunted down and killed. Now at last it was time for the princes to face Hengest and the Saxons.

One evening, Hengest looked out from the gates of Thancaster, in his small new kingdom of England, and there he saw the British lords coming, darkening the horizons with their banners. He saw Aurel and Uther and Eldol and many others besides, great warriors whose names he did not know; and it seemed to him that from the ground beneath his feet he heard the sound of women's voices, mourning and weeping. He turned to his own generals and servants.

'Our enemies are coming for us at last. See how their banners darken the sunset; there will be battle tomorrow. I do not fear battle; war has been my life, and my living. But tell me, what are those voices? They seem to come from within the women's quarters, in the longhouse behind us. But their language is strange. There is no word of Saxon in it, and no word of British, as far as I can tell.'

But the Saxons could not hear the voices, or tell Hengest what they meant, and Hengest never learned. The following morning he went out to battle.

That battle was fought in the valley of the Don, in Belin's Field, where some say Mexborough now stands. It lasted for two days. On the first day, when Hengest went out to fight, he was smiling and laughing as he rode. But on the first day of battle the English line was broken, and Hengest fled. By the end of the first day, Hengest was hemmed in within the gates of Thancaster. He spent a tense and miserable night. Again that night he heard the voices, but he knew better than to tell anyone about them, other than his closest friends. When he ventured out to battle on the second day, his smile was gone, and he was frowning. The ghostly women's voices were still gnawing at his ears.

And there, in the turmoil of battle on the second day, Hengest met Eldol of the Dragon-Hill, and fought with him hand to hand. Eldol overthrew Hengest by sheer chance, and seized him by the nosepiece of his helmet. He chained him, and led him prisoner before the two princes, Aurel and Uther, as he had promised; and the proud princes smiled, and gave the word, and Eldol slaughtered Hengest in front of them.

Hengest's enemies laid him in a Saxon grave: an earthen mound, in the shadow of his own stronghold. Some say the grave-mound stands in the shadow of Conisbrough Castle to this day. Then they burned his longhouse, and left its ruins deserted, and made an end of his little kingdom of England, before returning to London. Aurel became king, and Uther was king after him. Uther's son, the great Arthur, was king after Uther's death. Arthur was the greatest king of the old days, and he kept the Saxons out of Britain.

For many years afterwards, no fortress or stronghold stood on the hills above the rivers. But, when Arthur was gone, the Saxons remembered Hengest's old kingdom of England with fondness. They came back in strength, and they conquered the most part of the island. They called their new country England, the Land of the Hook, as once Hengest had called his little hide of land; and then they began to call themselves English. So they call themselves to this day.

Today, a town has grown up around the hill where Conan's stronghold and Hengest's longhouse once stood. The town still bears Conan's name: Conisbrough. And to this day the castle has an eerie reputation. Many ghosts are still said to haunt it. Rumours of women in white, and other strange presences, echo in and out of the white stone walls and battlements on the grassy hill between the rivers.

And, meanwhile, far away across the narrow seas, long after his death, King Conan is still getting his way. His language, the British of the ancient Britons, is still spoken in his old Half-Silent Realm of Little Britain, or Brittany. The language is still called Breton by many who know nothing of the ancient bloodshed behind the name; or its old brotherhood with those who dwell between the two rivers, the Don and the Dearne, in the very shadow of the ruins of Carconan on the Don.

The strongholds of the Don Valley are among the oldest settlements in South Yorkshire. Wincobank was an Iron Age hill fort; the Romans for-tified nearby Templeborough. These places have long evoked a sense of ancient mystery and splendour. Rumours abounded of buried treasure at Wincobank, and a widely quoted prophecy dating from 1662 states that:

When all the world shall be aloft
Then *Hallam-shire* shall be God's croft.
Winkabank and *Temple-brough*
Will buy all England through and through.

Following the end of Roman rule, Celtic British rulers reasserted their power, but soon faced Saxon encroachments; some fled in exile to Europe, but a British kingdom of Elmet, based around Leeds, endured for some time. The legends of Conan and Hengest, told by medieval writers, including Layamon and Geoffrey of Monmouth, reflect this Dark Age turbulence, but picture its action lower down the Don Valley, towards Conisbrough, the major urban centre of their own day. St Peter's church, Conisbrough, begun in the eighth century, is reckoned to be the oldest building in South Yorkshire, and contains an extraordinary twelfth-century carving of the legend of St George and the Dragon, within which sharp eyes will glimpse the familiar features of a foliate head, the famous 'Green Man'. Geoffrey identifies Conisbrough as the site of Hengest's death, close to the site of the battle at Maes Beli ('the field of Beli', said by some to be Mexborough; we have called it Belin's Field). Hengest's trick with the leather hide is a very common and widespread folk tale motif.

Elizabethan antiquarians such as William Camden and John Speed reproduced Geoffrey's story. Edmund Gibson's expanded 1722 edition of Camden's Britannia *reports that a mound, 'said by tradition*

St George and the Dragon, St Peter's church, Conisbrough

to be the burying-place of Hengist', was still to be seen before the castle gates. The idea was taken up by later antiquarians, including Surtees (quoted by Eastwood), and the Naylor brothers, while a 1931 pamphlet refers to a 'Hengist's Grave' nearby 'between Sprotborough and Melton on the Hill'.

Conisbrough's name, however, seems to come not from the Celtic name Conan, but from a mixture of two much younger languages, Norse and Old English – konungr burh, *'king's stronghold'.*

Conisbrough Castle as it stands today is Norman, built in the twelfth century. It is said to be the site of several hauntings, including a Grey Monk, and a White Lady. Doncaster author John Tomlinson wrote in 1860:

It is said that the castle [Conisbrough] was intended to have been built at Mexborough, but some contrary elves always came in the night and transported the materials to its present site. It is also currently reported that there are here two subterranean passages, one to Roche Abbey and the other to Tickhill Castle.

Anon. (n.d.), *The Barnburgh Legend: The Cat and Man* (Doncaster Local History Library); Eastwood 1865; Naylor 1916; Tomlinson 1860: 43; Wilson 1994: 27; Cf. Ray and Belfour 1813.

THE BATTLE OF BRUNANBURH

For many years the Don Valley region lay on a troubled boundary between Saxon and Viking territory; then the Vikings overran it. But in AD 937, the great West Saxon king Athelstan, son of Edward, and grandson of Alfred the Great, drove them back, winning a major victory against a huge coalition of his enemies. South Yorkshire has been suggested more than once as the site of the battle, called Brunanburh in Old English. Armitage Goodall suggested a site around Brinsworth (Magoun 1933). The historian Michael Wood (1999) has similarly suggested nearby Tinsley Wood.

A contemporary poem, recorded in the Anglo-Saxon Chronicle, *celebrates this pivotal English victory. This is our translation of the poem from the original Old English. The English king Athelstan and his brother Edmund, leading Mercian and West Saxon forces, are shown routing Olaf, king of the Viking settlement based around Dublin, and Olaf's ally, the Scottish king Constantine. We have taken the liberty of translating Brunanburh as Brinsford, from an early name of Brinsworth.*

In August 2014 we organised a storywalk around Tinsley Park Wood. Chatting about the battle – and the poem – on the 6A bus from Sheffield Interchange, we were informed by a fellow passenger to Darnall that the 'first king of England' was crowned in Sheffield and buried at Totley. Several fellow-passengers had heard the same tale, but nobody could remember the king's name. It was probably Egbert. The Anglo-Saxon Chronicle *records that in 827 King Egbert of Wessex was hailed at Dore as high king of Anglo-Saxon England. The Battle of Brunanburh shows his descendants, asserting his old claim in the face of a new enemy.*

937: This year
Athelstan, king, wielder of warriors,
bright gold-bringer, with Edmund his brother
in battle beside him, won glory abiding
in slaughter and sweat of the sword's edge
before Brinsford. They broke the shield-wall there,
hewed its hardwood with a hammer's harvest.
Where indeed would sons of Edward,
lords of his line, look, if not to war,
for warrant and safety from hateful hands
for home and hoard? Down came death
on the hordes of Scots and sea-thieves. They were doomed,
and they died indeed, and darkened the turf
with the sweat of their blood from sun's first rising
at morning – star of wonder shining,
God's bright candle over the ground –
until the light that the good Lord made
sank to its setting, over the field
of the slain, by spear and shaft and squandered shield,
Scot and Northman together all tangled,
worn and wasted. All the long day,

West Saxons in ranks and bands
hounded and hunted the few who fled,
harried and hacked at their hateful heels
with sword's edge. Our Mercian men
were no misers either at the grim trade
of wounds with hungry squadrons who crossed
the surging seas in Olaf's wake
to scavenge a battle, but died. They left
five dead on the field, five young kings
sleeping deep by the sword's edge, and seven besides
of Olaf's earls, and countless common
thieves and Scots; they made the king
rat and run to save the skins
of his little crew in his little ship.
So the ship put out to sea; so the king went out
over dark waters to save his life.
That counsellor, too, salvaged his wise old
head for his home in the north – King Constantine,
who has seen battles enough, but will never boast
of this one, which tore friends from his side,
robbed him by many deaths of his fellow-thieves
in the ranks of slaughter; even his own son
was left, abandoned, ground down with wounds
into a boyhood grave. No hunger
for joy at that war's outcome had
that old grey Scottish fox. As little had Olaf,
and little cause enough had his pitiful remnant
to gloat of their own skill in the work of battle
on the field of war, at the banner's approach,
at gathering of spears and meeting of heroes,
weaving of weapons on the death-field where
they met to play with us at the game of war;
for they ran from our hands back to their nailed ships,
the few that we left alive, to Dinsmere,
and made for Dublin over deep water,
and the land of the Irish, with anguished mind.

The brothers meanwhile, prince and king
side by glorious side, returned home,
to West Saxon land with hearts overflowing,
leaving a feast in their wake of cold
flesh for old black-cloak, the dark raven,
old horn-face; a feast for old shadow-cloak,
the white-backed eagle; a feast of carrion
for greedy hawk and wild grey
wolf of the wood. Since the old days
on this long green land, never yet did one
war ever leave more warriors stricken
so deep by the sword's edge; so say the books;
so say the wise; not since the years
when English Saxon first from the east
crossed the brine's back to the land of Britain,
those wise old war-makers, herding the strangers
westward, our warrior-fathers, here to win us a world.

DEADMAN'S HOLE

In 1955, Mr W.F. Smith of Kimberworth wrote of his childhood home, Dead Man's Lane, then situated in farmland:

I remember the garden we had at the far end of Dead Man's Lane, called Dead Man's Hole. They used to tell me it was called that name because of a battle fought in the time of the Romans, and that the dead were buried there. Dead Man's Hole was a place where wild ducks and other birds used to rest for the night on their flights.

Deadman's Hole Lane – to give it its current name – is now off Sheffield Road, immediately east of the M1 at Meadowhall. It is an industrial site.

Rotherham Advertiser, 12-1-1957 (RALS).

Deadman's Hole Lane, Sheffield

THE BLACK RAVEN

There are villages on the moorlands where it is still possible to hear a harassed mother threatening to give little Johnny to the Black Raven if he does not behave himself. The Black Raven was the Viking war flag.

A local writer recorded this in 1960. A century previously, Ingledew refers to the 'famous Reafen, or enchanted standard, in which the Danes put great confidence. It contained the figure of a raven, which had been inwoven, by the three sisters of Hinguar and Hubba, with many magical incantations.' Its movements, he says, were believed to foretell good or bad fortune in forthcoming battles.

Ingledew 1860: 14n; Smith 1960: 78.

2

THE FORESTS

THE FOREST OF ELMET

King Richard, called Lionheart, was famous for two things: his greed and his temper. Hunting alone suited his dark temperament well, and so one day he went out from Tickhill Castle, ranging north towards the Don. Coming near Wadworth, south of the river, he put up a deer. She was a hind, a beautiful animal, and he spurred his horse, and set off in hot pursuit.

All that day he followed his prey through the chases and wild places. As the day grew old, he ran her towards Barnsdale Bar, near Wentbridge. There, on field and common beyond the forest's edge, the starving villagers were still toiling in the last of the daylight, trying to scrape a living from the unforgiving earth.

The fat deer broke cover and darted out into the open. The villagers eyed the great beast ravenously. They scarcely glanced at the wealthy huntsman staring at them from the edge of the forest. They dropped their tools, and their hands went to their knives, and as one man, they began to move in on the fat deer, to cut off her escape. Their thoughts went to the wives and children who could feast on the meat and make warm shoes from the leather.

But the last thing the king wanted was to spoil his day's sport for commoners. He rode out from the eaves of the forest with a great cry. The villagers' hunger-trance was broken, and every head turned to see the king lifting up his head to show his diadem, and shouting in a loud voice, 'No man shall kill that beast but me!'

Quietly the knives were sheathed, and the villagers' hands returned to their tools, and they turned back to their work in bitter silence. Their backs were still turned to the king as he hunted the deer into Wentbridge and out. Wentbridge remained hungry.

So Wentbridge lost the deer, and insult was shortly added to injury, for shortly afterwards a dispute came to court between a villager and the lord of the manor, over hunting and foraging rights on the common and in the forest. On the day that the case came to court, it was starting to look as if the judge might rule in favour of the peasant, but the lord's lawyer was an enterprising soul, and he had heard the gossip about the deer, and he thought he had nothing to lose by claiming that, legally, the whole forest was already out of bounds to the villagers. Did the forest not belong already to the king, and to him alone? Hadn't His Majesty already commanded (the lawyer argued) that none should kill the forest deer but himself? Hadn't the villagers heard his command and freely obeyed it, refusing to touch the deer, hungry though they were?

There was a moment's pause in court. The villagers had to admit that everything had happened as the lawyer had said. The judge nodded. And so the lawyer – much to his own surprise – won his case.

After that, the matter was settled forever. The rich, dark forest of Elmet became a royal hunting reserve. In the generations that followed, many were to die of cold and hunger who might have survived by hunting for its game and foraging for its firewood; and the great silent woodland was little enough appreciated by anyone, even by the king, except perhaps as an occasional plaything.

We learned this story from Paul Davenport of Maltby. Tickhill Castle was a typical Anglo-Norman timber fortress, rebuilt in stone in the twelfth century. It was held by Ranulf, Earl of Chester, a great warlord and ballad-hero in his own right, now largely forgotten, but once mentioned in the same breath as Robin Hood by authors such as the priest-poet William Langland. The woodlands of south and west Yorkshire were called the 'forest of Elmet' by Bede.

ROCHE ABBEY

In the days of the great forests, twelve monks came from Newminster in Northumberland, looking for a wild and remote place to build a new abbey, far from the comforts and temptations of court and town life. Their leader, Brother Durand, carried a staff in the form of the cross of Christ as he walked.

Roche Abbey

Far from home, hungry, cold and weary, they came at last to a wild valley thickly wooded and hemmed in by a craggy wall of living rock. Time and chance and weather had shaped one outcrop of the cliff into the form of a rough cross. They took it as a sign, and knelt in prayer, thankful that they had found their place. The new abbey took its name from the rock that gave the monks their vision of the cross. So it was called Roche Abbey. In time the abbey found riches from the rock, for the monks quarried it.

Cistercian monks arrived in Yorkshire in the twelfth century, during a Europe-wide revival of monastic life and learning. This legend of the foundation of the abbey of St Maria de Rupe (Mary of the Rock) – that is, Roche Abbey – is recorded by James H. Aveling. When the monasteries were dissolved, and the Crown agents Leigh and Layton visited Roche Abbey in 1537, they reported that the monks still worshipped a nearby rock on which there was an image of the crucifix.

Aveling 1870 (RALS).

BARNBURGH: CAT AND MAN

The Cresacres had been lords in Barnburgh since the Conqueror's time. They lived at Barnburgh Hall, within a spur of Barnsdale Forest and, although the hall is gone now, the family are still remembered. About five hundred years ago, the head of the family was Sir Percival Cresacre. It is said to be Sir Percy's remains that lie at rest in the Cresacre chapel in St Peter's church, under their famous oak-wood effigy, the knight himself having met with a death so strange that the story of it is told to this day.

Percy Cresacre was a veteran of the Crusades – but he had seen little fighting and, like many knights, he was not really a great warrior. He was more at home as the lord of wide estates, a manager of men, and an administrator of land. The family had many concerns in the district, and Percy was often to be seen riding early and late on its roads, going to and from the hall, on one errand or another.

St Peter's church, Barnburgh

Among his concerns was the Doncaster branch of the Templars. The great order of crusader-knights held land and privileges all over England, and in many places beyond. Over the years, many excitable souls have hinted that the Templars were heretics, or witches, or guardians of the Holy Grail, or some such thing as that; perhaps they were, but if the senior Templars really did nurse such secrets, Percy himself was a country knight, far too humble in rank to suspect anything of them. As far as Doncaster and the Cresacres were concerned, the Templar meetings at Greyfriars were more like the local branch of the Rotary Club or the Country Landowners' Association.

No mystical secrets were playing on Percy's mind the night he rode home from a meeting of the Doncaster Templars, down Ludwell Hill close to Melton. His thoughts were taken up with subscriptions, fees, falling rents, rising wages, and the cost of building works in St Peter's, which were always high for the Cresacres, because they always hated to be outdone in their generosity by the other big local families. Pondering on these things, more or less idly, he rode by the eaves of Melton Wood, towards the crossroads where the road began to climb the hill. In the shadowy undergrowth that hemmed the road, he could hear the beasts of the night, but it would be a strange thing at that hour if he could not have heard them. There is little silence in nature.

So there was no warning before the burning pain struck him, and a heavy weight in the darkness sent him reeling. He grappled for his sword, spurring his horse as it reared, and twisted in the saddle to face his unknown attacker.

Even today, rumours of great cats haunt the field and roads of the district. Already, in Percy Cresacre's days, they were rare – the Cresacre gamekeepers and foresters had seen to that. But they were no rumour. Percy was under attack, and, twisting round to face his assailant, he found himself staring, amazed, into the hissing, spitting snarl of a great wild wood-cat, the first he had ever seen.

He was startled – and annoyed. His first instinct was to spur his horse and outride it, and maybe give the thing a couple of fresh wounds to remember him by. And then, once he was safely home, order a good bath, offer a decent bounty per catskin for his huntsmen and foresters, and rid the forest of these vermin once and for all.

But the obscene weight of the thing clung to him as he spurred his horse on, and his well-bred palfrey, Winifred, was no warhorse. She bolted over Ludwell Spring, and then reared in the road at St Helen's Stream, throwing him.

The sword fell from his hand. Percy was left sprawling on his back in the grit of the road, wincing in pain and fighting for breath and balance.

The horse neighed, and bolted in terror, clattering up the hill towards the village.

And then the thing was bearing down on him again.

Percy Cresacre rolled aside frantically. In the frenzy of the moment, it seemed to Percy as if the cat seemed to be driven by something more than hunger or fear.

The cat landed on its feet beside him, wheeled, and lunged again. The man groped for the sword where it lay, and kicked and stabbed desperately. Stung, the shadowy beast withdrew a pace. Percy scrambled to his feet. The cat gaped and snarled and spat in the shadows. But for the moment the man had it at bay.

Far behind them, the terrified horse was disappearing, riderless, up the moonlit road, making for Barnburgh.

Percy was stranded, alone and on foot, facing a hand-to-hand fight with a seemingly implacable enemy.

For a moment, the two faced off against each other, and Percy caught his breath. He knew now that he would have to back slowly up the hill, parrying and defending until the thing fled. But he would make it home and have nothing worse to worry about than finding a way to laugh off his misadventure when the household got to hear of it, as they surely would.

Holding his sword on guard, and keeping his eye on the hissing beast crouched before him, he began to back slowly up the road.

The thing came after him, prowling on its belly. Percy was just beginning to get into something like a stride when it suddenly readied itself, and sprang again. With horrific suddenness the wood-cat was at his throat again, in his face. For a moment, cat and man were face to face in the dark. Its eyes were wide with a strange, cold, ageless light. His own burning blood flowed under its claws and fangs. He seized the blade of the sword with both hands, and parried the lunge at close quarters.

The blade of his sword gashed the cat's face deep. It hissed, and writhed, and fell. Percy almost cheered.

It will not be too proud to run now, he told himself. *Beasts are wiser than men.*

But the cat did not run. It recoiled, turned smoothly round, gathered its strength and balance, and came at him again, and again, as remorseless as lightning in a storm. He fended its huge weight off with kicks and blows, and it slid back, rallied, and sprang again. He braced himself. They grappled again. The man's blood had flowed at the first blow, and now the tatters of his rich coat were soaked.

Percy Cresacre's head began to swim. He felt something worse than pain in his own bloody wounds; he could feel the cat's fury, worming deep into his flesh like a loathsome disease.

And with that thought, Percy Cresacre began to feel afraid.

Man of peace though he was by choice, Percy still knew what it meant to lose blood in a hand-to-hand fight. Even if he made it to the village, if he came too slow, or too late, and too weak, then he would be coming home only to sicken and die, slowly, as Robin Hood himself had died, in the songs and stories of Barnsdale that Percy had known well all his life. And that meant one thing: the cat had the power to kill him. The thing was mad, and that meant that the fight in the moonlight was a fight to the death.

And so the man swallowed his disgust and faced the cat again; and the cat faced the man, and each in the moonlight looked long and hard into the face of death.

And all that night, cat and man fought their lonely fight, across Harlington Common and up the hill to Barnburgh, across road and river. The hours passed, and the man began to feel as if there had never been a time that he had not been staring into the eyes, the snarling teeth. It seemed like a dream. At times, Percy felt that he was watching another man fighting the cat: in the middle of his own terror, he felt strangely calm, even as the prospect of a safe return home became ever more remote. They fought on, and every so often Percy's thoughts would flicker to the warm rooms and friendly lights of his distant home, and the memory struck him as the memory of a strange place. A foreign place. He no longer seemed to belong there. He belonged here: fighting a wild cat under the moon, in the shadows of the trees.

As the moon sank, the cat's blood lay mingled with the man's all along the road; their movements grew slower and their breathing heavier.

Day began to dawn unseen around them as they fought: slowly, peacefully, little by little, the darkness lifted and the dawn gathered in the east.

At last, on the outskirts of Barnburgh, the exhausted knight faced his mortal enemy one last time: an angry, hissing animal, wounded and dishevelled, scarcely bigger in the daylight than a farm cat.

And then, for the first time, Percy spoke aloud to the dauntless animal. His voice sounded hoarse and strange in his own ears.

'Have I shed all this blood,' he asked aloud, 'for thee?'

The moonlit gleam was gone from the cat's green eyes, but still it hissed and snarled. It drew itself up, its ears flat. It was ready to pounce again.

And then, at last, in that moment, Percy saw the only way that the fight could end.

Strangely, the last of his fear left him, and his heart grew light. He wanted to laugh, but he had no breath left. So, in a hoarse whisper, he spoke again to the cat, for the last time.

'Well, look, here we are in Barnburgh – I have made it home at last. When I set out last night,' he said – and he scarcely knew why he spoke – 'I thought that I ruled the forest. But I was wrong. I was a rich man then: a man of property. Today I leave the world empty-handed, forever. But I die as my fathers died, sword in hand. And now when I meet them, I know they will not be ashamed. You, my enemy, fought naked and unarmed, with the heart of a hunter, and you fought in your own place, for your own territory; and you have brought down a rich man in his pride. So of the two of us, you are the greater. Come, then, little cat. Not far to go now. Let us go home.'

Percy Cresacre was found that morning by one of the priest's servants, alerted by the search party from the hall, where the riderless horse had come in the night. The knight had made it as far as the church porch. It seemed that he had crawled there on purpose, as if to make sure that he would be found.

Wonder struck the grieving servants when they found him, and silence fell on them. For dead at their master's feet lay a wild wood-cat, bigger by far than any they had ever seen, or heard of. No such wild beast had ever ventured into Barnburgh by daylight before. Even in the first shock of grief, even in death they saw that the beast was magnificently cruelly beautiful – beautiful as wild animals are. But its ribs were smashed. In his death-agony, Percy Cresacre had crushed the wood-cat to death with his boot, against the wall of the porch.

They laid Sir Percy Cresacre in the tomb in the Cresacre chapel, in the corner of St Peter's church. In the dark oak of the tomb, they carved the figures of cat and man, lying as they were found. The carving can still be seen today, just as the story it tells can still be heard; and still, on the porch stones of St Peter's, so they say, is the stain of their mingled blood.

The story of the Cat and Man (the cat is always mentioned first, and no one ever seems to refer to 'the Cat and the Man') is widely told today. There are many variations in detail, which we have drawn on for our version, but, as Colin Howes of Doncaster Museum noted, not all of them fit the geography of the area. Fiona Firth (2003) quoted Colin Howes to the effect that the tale's known sources are twofold: Bingley's Animal Biography *of 1802; and Hatfield's 'Village Sketches' in the* Doncaster Gazette *of 1849.*

How long the story was told before that is a matter of surmise. It is not implausible that a knight called Cresacre might have been attacked by a wild wood-cat on a ride from Doncaster to Barnburgh. The lynx was not exterminated in Britain until the seventeenth century. But the real Percy Cresacre was not a crusader, and the tomb in St Peter's is probably that of his ancestor, Thomas. The wooden effigy shows a cat crouched at the feet of the knight, and Notes and Queries *in 1899 recorded that the 'cat-a-mountain' was the crest of the Cresacre family. But the creature on the effigy is not a house cat, or even a wild cat, but a lion – not an uncommon detail on tombs of the time. Numerous legends exist accounting for details of effigies, and the Shropshire story of Old Scriven of Brompton, cited by Jennifer Westwood and Jacqueline Simpson (2006 (2005): 614), features a knight killing a lion in a manner very similar to the story of Sir Percy Cresacre killing the cat. Clifford Ward (n.d.), in a history of St Peter's available at the church, suggests, plausibly, that the story arose after the Reformation, and was inspired by the mysterious details of the effigy itself.*

*Ted Armstrong (1980) argued that the legend was originally 'a means of remembering the stones and centres of the earthly powers which the Templars knew of and tried to subdue ... The conflict (*Kat*) over the power of the stone (*Maen*) became the legend of the Cat and Man.' Bob Chiswick's song 'The Ballad of the Cat and Man' was recorded in 1987 by his band Off the Cuff (1987). John Tunney (1992) mentioned that the story has also been interpreted as a garbled memory of the Battle of Maes Beli (see 'Carconan on the Don', Chapter 1). Ted Hughes – a Mexborough lad – references the story in his well-known poem 'Esther's Tomcat'. In 1993, it was reported that residents*

*of Darfield recalled that the fight began in that village, on Cat Hill.
Finally, Chris Ingram tells us that Barnburgh schools still abound with
rumours relating to the buried treasure of the Cresacres.*

*The hall passed by marriage from the Cresacres to the son of
Henry VIII's famous chancellor, Thomas More. John Tunney mentions
that the Mores left Barnburgh in the 1820s. Barnburgh Hall was later
acquired by the National Coal Board, which demolished it in 1969.*

Barnburgh St Peter's Mothers' Union 1993 (Doncaster Local History
Library); *Notes and Queries* No. 2, Vol. 1 (September 1899): 84.

3

ROBIN HOOD
OF BARNSDALE

South Yorkshire is the setting for many of the oldest-known Robin Hood stories. In these late medieval ballads, Robin appears as a highway robber active on Ermine Street (later the Great North Road, and later still the A1, sometimes referred to in the ballads as Watling Street). He ventures regularly to and from Nottingham (although the Great North Road would not have taken him there). His home territory is the area north-west of Doncaster, which still bears the name Barnsdale.

Pre-eminent among the early ballads is the so-called 'Gest of Robyn Hode', no. 117 in F.J. Child's collection (1965 (1882–98)) (gest meaning 'deeds' or 'acts'). This long narrative, apparently stitched together from several shorter episodes, survives in a handful of later fifteenth-century printed editions from London and Antwerp. 'Robin Hood and the Potter' survives in a manuscript that dates from about 1500. Shorter, and markedly more violent, is 'Robin Hood and Guy of Gisborne', which survives only in a mid-seventeenth-century manuscript, possibly somewhat garbled; fragmentary references in older sources have led scholars to conclude that the story is late medieval.

In the old ballads, Robin Hood appears as the character we know today – in some respects. He is a commoner, not an exiled nobleman; he has no lover, no Maid Marian; he is religious, and particularly devoted to the Virgin Mary; he sometimes claims allegiance to a

King Edward, but knows nothing of any King John or Richard; and he robs from the rich – or some of them – but he does not give to the poor.

The full text of the ballad 'Gest of Robin Hood' consists of a whopping 456 stanzas. We have told the story in prose, as best we could. With the other ballads, we stay as close to the original ballad verse as we could readably get. We have done our best to restore the circumstantial detail of Robin's encounter with Guy of Gisburn; Robin's macabre desecration of Guy's corpse is not fully explained in the surviving ballad text, which seems garbled in places: it has even been explained as an act of 'ritual' violence.[24] But Robin's motive at this point is to fake his own death and go to the Sheriff disguised as Guy. We deduce that he is improvising a grisly prop: rendering Guy's head unrecognisable, in order to pass it off as his own. Also, we note that the original ballad rhymes Gisborne with turne – not sworne, as in Bishop Percy's text,[25] which seems to have been edited by the good bishop, as if to avoid the mildly profane 'curst turne' (i.e., cursed or evil deed).[26] We have therefore assumed that the original rhyme was with turne. This allows us to infer that Sir Guy, a forester, hails from Gisburn (formerly in West Yorkshire), which has more than one old forest. The nearest places we know called Gisborne, to rhyme with 'sworn', are in Australia and New Zealand.

*South Yorkshire has long abounded in Robin Hood locations. Seventeenth-century antiquarians recall that Robin Hood was supposedly born in the Loxley Valley, just north-west of Sheffield. In his 1637 work (*An Exact and Perfect Survey and View of the Manor of Sheffield, with Other Lands*), John Harrison pinpointed Robin Hood's alleged birthplace as Little Haggas Croft, now a green field on the edge of Loxley village. In the later Middle Ages, someone around*

24 'Robin Hood and Guy of Gisborne', University of Rochester TEAMS Middle English Text Series http://d.lib.rochester.edu/teams/text/robin-hood-and-guy-of-gisborne-introduction, accessed 10-1-2015.

25 Percy, Thomas, *Reliques of Ancient English Poetry* (London: J.M. Dent & Sons, 1910 (1906)). www.archive.org/stream/percysreliquesof01percuoft#page/120/mode/2up, accessed 10-1-2015.

26 'Robin Hood and Guy of Gisborne', accessed 10-1-2015.

Loxley really does seem to have been called Robin Hood. But he was not the first to bear this name, and it may have been a nickname, perhaps connected to a local tradition of Robin Hood pageants or plays. In troubled times, in the aftermath of the Peasants' Revolt, it may even have been the alias of a wanted man. Loxley's Robin Hood Inn was built in 1799.

Barnsdale Bar is still a junction on the A1 close to Wentbridge. There is still a Barnsdale Wood nearby, and W.R. Mitchell (1970: 24–7) mentions a tradition that Robin got married at Campsall. Robin's favourite lookout point in these stories, which in the ballads he calls the 'Saylis', has been tentatively pinpointed since the nineteenth century to several locations along this stretch of the A1, where it crosses the Went and Skell rivers. A blue plaque in Wentbridge itself now identifies the Saylis lookout point as Brockadale, a deep-sided gorge on the edge of the village. We take this to be the case. The Great North Road, now the A1(M), now vaults the gorge over an award-winning 1961 concrete viaduct, but even this has failed to dissipate Brockadale's air of sudden seclusion and mystery.

And here – or nearby, in a layby on the southbound A1 outside Burghwallis – stands Robin Hood's Well. Mitchell mentions references to 'the stone of Robert Hode' going back to 1332, which may be the same place, and the Doncaster Chronicle *in 1914 reported that it was thought to be 'Robertis place', a centre of entertainment to which bored French noblemen, prisoners in the Hundred Years' War, were always skiving off to from Pontefract, until Henry V told the Bishop of Durham to put a stop to it. Later, and for a small fee, Stuart-age travellers could take a drink from the well, sit in the stone chair, or take part in other fake-medieval rituals, and the well was popular enough to be furnished with a stone canopy by John Vanbrugh, which still stands. Similar rites were practised by the Naylor brothers in the later nineteenth century, and the Robin Hood Inn was a nearby coach-stop, so the tradition seems to have lasted. The Skell has been diverted and the original well is now dry. The Vanbrugh canopy has been moved from the original site of the well to accommodate the dual carriageway, and it stands now in a lay-by off the main road.*

Cannon Hall, Cawthorne

Little John's grave is still pointed out in Hathersage churchyard. His armour and weapons are said to have been kept at Cannon Hall, the Spencer-Stanhope family seat, at Cawthorne near Barnsley. Charles Pratt (1882) noted a story published in 1865 from the testimony of a fellow clergyman, Charles Spencer-Stanhope, regarding these items – a bow, arrows and a chain-mail shirt. The Spencers removed them from their previous home in Hathersage church, Derbyshire, where the antiquarian Elias Ashmole (1617–1692) had heard something of them years before. The family felt entitled to move the items presumably because Hathersage was once part of the Spencer family estate. Spencer-Stanhope describes the bow as six feet of spliced yew, a classic English longbow, inscribed with the name of a Colonel Naylor, and the date 1715, supposedly marking the last occasion of its use. But Spencer-Stanhope's account of the mail-shirt seems to derive from family hearsay relating to an object he had never seen. In 1888, in notes now in the Lucy Broadwood collection, W.R. Holland described the items at Cannon Hall as Little John's

'bow, cap and chain mail'. The mail-shirt seems to have perished –
Spencer-Stanhope says it had been 'much reduced' by 'people stealing
rings from it for memorials' – but in 1970, W.R. Mitchell published
a photograph of the bow, and wrote that it 'is owned by Mr Simon
Fraser, of Horsforth'.

Until its death in the later nineteenth century, a trysting tree stood
in Kiveton Wood, a bluebell wood on Kiveton Lane just south of
Todwick (Robins and Sickler n.d.: 57). This is remembered locally as
a meeting place for Robin and his men, and the inspiration for the
'Trysting-tree in the Harthill-walk' in Walter Scott's Ivanhoe. It was
replaced in 1901 by a sapling of the more famous Major Oak, and the
site was marked by a plaque in 1974.

The former RAF Finningley was reopened for civil aviation
as Doncaster Robin Hood Airport in 2005, and has a statue of the
outlaw installed in the passenger terminal.

Other place names associated with Robin Hood are scattered
through West and North Yorkshire, Derbyshire, the Borders, and also
the West Country.

Doncaster Chronicle 29-5-1914 (Doncaster Local Studies Library);
Rotherham Advertiser 3-5-1974, 24-5-1974 (RALS); EFDSS archive, Lucy
Broadwood Manuscript Collection (LEB/5/489) (Full English Archive
Collections: www.vwml.org/record/LEB/5/489, accessed 4-1-2015).

ROBIN HOOD'S BIRTH AND OUTLAWRY

Robert Locksley, born in Bradfield parish, in Hallamshire
(S. Yorkshire), wounded his stepfather to death at plough: fled into
the woods, and was relieved by his mother till he was discovered.
Then he came to Clifton upon Calder, and came acquainted with
Little John …

Roger Dodworth, Sloane MS – Bodleian Library, Dodsworth
MS 160, fo. 64b, quoted www.robinhoodlegend.com/
the-many-robin-hoods-5, accessed 29-12-2012.

ROBIN HOOD AND GUY OF GISBURN

When trees were green, and branches bright,
and leaves were large and long,
and small birds in the morning air sang out their lovely song,
and woodwalls sang unceasingly upon the oaken leaf,
then Robin Hood woke up one day,
his head bowed down with grief.

'I had this nightmare, John,' he said, 'I dreamt it in the night;
I dreamt I met a forester who challenged me to fight.
He beat me, and he tied me up, and took my bow from me;
I'm Robin Hood of Barnsdale, and revenged I'll surely be!'
'Revenged for what?' said Little John. 'A dream is just a dream.
Dreams are illusions, truth is truth, no matter how things seem.'
'That dream was real,' cried Robin Hood, 'so come, John, follow me,
and when we find that forester, revenged for real I'll be!'

Robin and John put green hoods on, and hunting gone are they.
They searched until the noonday sun stood high above the day,
and then in truth they found him, leaning against a tree:
a sword and dagger by his side which many a man had slain;
a woodsman in a horse-hide hood – top and tail and mane.

'Wait here, master,' growled Little John, 'beneath this greenwood tree;
I'll go and ask that stranger what his business here may be.'
'What, me wait here?' said Robin Hood. 'You think I wouldn't mind
sending a proxy on ahead, and cringe here, far behind?
Not likely. And you've got some nerve, the way I hear you speak.
And if it wouldn't dent my bow, your head today I'd break!'

The two friends fell to argument, and off in a rage stormed John,
and back to Barnsdale made his way – the paths he knew each one;
but when he came to Barnsdale, great horror there he found;
for there his friends, the thieves, all lay,
all murdered on the ground.

Red Will alone was living, running off by stock and stone.
The Sheriff's men were after him, ten well-armed men on one.
'I'll shoot one shot,' says Little John, 'By Christ, with might and main!
I'll make Red Will, that runs so fast, stroll easy home again.'

So John picked up a bow of yew, and made ready to shoot;
the bow was raw unseasoned wood and splintered to John's foot.
'God damn that raw unseasoned wood, that ever it made a tree!
Today that bow has been my death, when it my life should be!'

John shot, but it was loosely shot; the arrow flew in vain.
It struck one of the Sheriff's men – so William Trent was slain,
and worse it went for William Trent than torture on the rack;
for he died there, in an outlaw's lair, with an arrow in his back –

but so it's said, when men are met, more strength have six than three;
and Little John was beaten down, and bound up to a tree.
'I'll drag you up hill and down dale, and hang you on the hill,'
the Sheriff said. 'Perhaps you will,' snarled John, 'if that's God's will.'

Let's speak no more of Little John who's tied up to a tree;
let's speak of Guy and Robin Hood out in the forest free,
where these two foresters soon met, under the oak-tree bough;
and telling all their business then is all our business now.

The stranger gave a greeting, and Robin answered free:
'With such a bow upon your back, an archer you must be.'
'I am at times,' the stranger said; 'not when I've work to do.'
'What work is that?' asked Robin Hood. 'For I have business too.'

'I hunt an outlaw,' said the man; 'they call him Robin Hood;
if luck would bring him here today, I'd say my luck was good.'
'If he was here,' said Robin Hood, 'and met you here today,
you'd see who was the better man before you went your way!

'So let's just try some archery for pastime as we go –
we might run into Robin after that. You never know.'
And so they cut the branches down that grew beneath the briar,
at twelve score yards they set the stakes, to shoot to their desire.

'Which of us two,' said Robin Hood, 'shall shoot his shot the first?'
'Not I, by God,' the stranger said; 'let's see you do your worst.'
The first good shot that Robin shoots, an inch from the mark it goes;
no matter how the stranger shoots, he'll never come so close.

The first good shot the stranger shot, it made the garland shake;
but Robin was the better shot; he split the very stake.
'Tell me your name,' the stranger said, 'man of the greenwood shaws!'
'Not I, by God,' said Robin Hood, 'till you have told me yours.'

'I live by dale and down,' he said, 'and done many an ill turn;
and if you want to know my name, I'm Guy of good Gisburn.'
'And I'm from Barnsdale,' Robin said; 'to names I give no thought;
because my name is Robin Hood; you've found the man you've sought!'

If then a while you could have watched, then you'd have seen a sight:
the way these forest-hunters fought with bloody blades and bright,
the way these forest-hunters fought two hours that summer's day,
since neither Guy nor Robin had a mind to run away,

till Robin took a reckless turn and stumbled to his knee,
and Guy was stronger on his feet – at Robin's ribs struck he.
'Sweet Mary mild!' cried Robin Hood, 'who watches by the way!
It never was man's destiny to die before his day –'

So trusting in our Lady's grace, he soon jumped up again,
and came back, with a backhand stroke that left his rival slain.
He hacked Guy's neck and grabbed his head, and set it on a stake:
'You who did treason all your life, a traitor's end you'll make!'

Then Robin drew his Irish knife and cut Sir Guy's dead face,
till never a man from woman born could tell whose head it was.
'Now back you come with me, Sir Guy, since now it's plain to see
I've carved your face so handsome, you could even pass for me!'

Robin pulled off his hood of green, and wrapped the bloody head,
and wore the horse-hide hood himself, and this is what he said:
'Your bows, your arrows, head and all, I'll borrow and I'll bear
from here right back to Barnsdale – since I guess the Sheriff's there.'

He set Guy's horn to his own mouth, and a loud blast did blow;
and the proud Sheriff heard that blast, in Barnsdale far below.
'Listen!' the Sheriff cried for joy, 'The news sounds like it's good.
That horn-call is the passing-bell that tolls for Robin Hood.

'Out there I hear Sir Guy's horn blow – and see down there beside –
here comes Sir Guy of Gisburn in his hood of horse's hide!'
The horse-hide hood cloaked Robin from his head down to his feet,
and out of the wood came Robin Hood, and at the Sheriff's feet
he threw the bloody head and cloak, the Sheriff for to greet.

'Well done, Sir Guy of Gisburn! Ask your reward from me!'
'I want no gold or silver, no, nor land, nor livery;
but now I've killed the master, only let me kill the man;
and let it be said all England through that I killed Little John!'

'You must be mad,' the Sheriff shrugged, 'to take no gold from me;
but since your asking is so bad, well granted shall it be.'
When John first saw the bloody head, the tear was in his eye;
but when he heard sweet Robin's voice, see how his tears did dry,

and Robin came to Little John, with knife to cut the band,
but all the seven score Sheriff's men crept close around to stand:
'Stand back, you fools,' called Robin Hood, 'why listen in so near?
None but the executioner the thief's last words should hear.'

Then Robin drew his Irish knife and loosed John hand and foot,
and put Guy's bow in John's great hands for Little John to shoot,
and Little John took Guy's long bow and arrows rusted red;
the Sheriff soon caught sight of that, and turned and quickly fled,

cried for his house in Nottingham, and quickly ran away,
and so did all his company; not one behind would stay;
but still, for all his running, there was nothing he could do,
for Little John shot one swift bolt, and cut his heart in two.

ROBIN HOOD AND THE POTTER

THE PROUD POTTER

Now listen and I'll tell you, friends, and neighbours kind and good,
about the world's best archer, and his name was Robin Hood;
and that was what they called him, and his life was free and wild,
but he never hurt a woman, for the love of Mary mild.

In summer when the leaves are green and little birds all sing,
an outlaw's life among the trees, it is a pleasant thing,
and Robin chanced to watch the roads one sunny market day,
and there he saw a potter's cart, rattling down the way.

'There's that proud potter,' Robin said; 'I know him well enough.
He comes down every market-day – why don't we steal his stuff?'
'Oh no, not him,' said Little John, 'bad luck to him therefore!
I fought him once at Wentbridge, and my bones are still quite sore.

'So forty pounds,' said Little John, 'I'll gladly give away
to any who can make him pay for passing by today.'
'So forty more,' said Robin Hood, 'I'll gladly give likewise
if I don't make him pay, right now, right here before your eyes.'

These two then paid the wagers down; the others made a book,
and into the road bold Robin Hood three long, lean strides he took.
He grabbed the bridle of the horse. The potter showed no fear.
The cart stood still. The potter roared: 'Hey, stranger! What's this here?'

'You come down every market-day beneath the greenwood leaves,
but you've never given tuppence to the poor old forest-thieves.'
'So what?' the potter answered him. 'And who, by Christ, are you?'
'I'm Robin Hood. This road is mine. And, friend, your toll is due.'

'I'm paying nought,' the potter said, 'so let that bridle go,
or you'll be paying tolls to me. That won't be cheap, you know.'
He rummaged back among his pots and drew a stout staff out,
and leapt right down from off the cart, and brandished it about,

and Robin, with his sword in hand and small shield by his side,
stepped up to him – the potter shouted, 'Outlaw, stand aside!'
They fought together then, like dogs. It was a sight to see.
The band of thieves cheered Robin on beneath the greenwood tree,

and Little John yelled Robin on, and urged him still to stand;
the potter swung his staff and knocked the shield from Robin's hand,
and Robin bent to pick it up, and scrambled on the ground;
the potter stove his kidneys in, and Robin Hood went down.

And when the band of thieves saw that,
they laughed and cheered no more;
but Little John ran out to fight, as Robin writhed and swore;
the band of thieves hedged Robin round, and hemmed the potter in,
and Little John laughed grimly: 'Christ, this bet I'm going to win.

'You bet me forty pounds, Robin, you'd beat this lad today.
And now he's got you pissing blood. So who's won, would you say?'
Meanwhile the potter cursed and swore: 'Sweet Jesus Christ!' cried he.
'The outlaw's got his mates to help. And there's just one of me.'

'Back off him, lads,' groaned Robin Hood, 'for what he says is right.
He's one against two dozen, and that's no fair way to fight.
So, potter – no hard feelings, friend –
come change your cloaks with me.
You stay here. I'll go off to town, and sell your pottery!'

'You? Trade my pots?' the potter cried, 'I'll say this to your face:
a slob like you won't sell one pot in any market-place.'
'You reckon so?' cried Robin Hood, 'Then God refuse me grace
if I don't sell your stock out, in the nearest market-place.'

When Little John heard Robin's words, he groaned and tore his hair:
'The nearest market's Nottingham. They've a Sheriff there …'
'The Sheriff? Sod him,' Robin said, 'we fear no Sheriffs here.'
He climbed the cart and took the reins, and down the road did steer,

and Robin went to Nottingham, the potter's pots to sell;
the potter put a green cloak on, and went with thieves to dwell;
and Robin Hood to Nottingham quite happily has gone.
So ends the first part of this tale. The best is yet to come.

THE POTTER ROBIN HOOD

When Robin came to Nottingham (the truth to plainly tell),
he tied the horse and cart up, and he took the pots to sell,
and in the city market-place those pots stood plain to see,
while Robin shouted: 'Ladies! Gents! Come buy one, get one free!'

He piled pots high and sold pots cheap; he sold them for a song;
the people shook their heads and smiled: 'He'll not be trading long!'
He sold them at three shillings, when the worst could have got five,
and women laughed behind their hands: 'His business won't survive!'

Close by the Sheriff's town-house door stood Robin's market-stall,
and wives and widows flocked to him, and bought pots, pans and all,
till Robin sold the pots out – he was down to his last five,
and those he gave away for free, to the Sheriff's smart new wife.

The Sheriff's wife stood at the door: 'Thanks, potter,' then said she;
   'I'll buy my pots from you alone, since I've had five for free!'
And Robin smiled and thanked her, and he seemed so very able,
   she asked him in that night to dine at the Sheriff's high table.

Then Robin smiled a second time, and grinned so very wide,
   and off to meet the Sheriff then those two they went inside,
and Robin came to the great hall, and there the Sheriff stood;
   but prouder stood his visitor, the potter Robin Hood.

'This potter gave us five free pots!' declared the Sheriff's wife,
   'We must have him to dinner.' Robin thought, 'This is the life.'
And as they sat at dinner, every guest in their degree,
   the talk around the table turned to sport and archery;

an open shooting-contest, just an hour or two to go,
   with forty pounds of silver for the best man at the bow.
The potter listened to the talk, and never a word said he.
The one thought in his head was, 'That prize is meant for me!'

When each had had their fill of all the meat and bread and wine,
   they went off to that contest, and stood ready at the line;
the Sheriff's men shot fair and free, but wide and high and low;
   not one could shoot much closer than the length of half a bow.

Then up spoke the proud potter, and he shouted fair and free:
   'By Christ, if I could get a bow, I'd show you archery!'
'Is that a fact?' the Sheriff snapped. 'Then borrow a bow, please;
   why should a potter, after all, shoot any worse than these?'

The Sheriff called a servant, and he told him bows to bring;
   and on the best bow that he had the potter set a string.
'And now let's see how well you shoot the best bow in my hall!'
'For Christ's sake,' muttered Robin Hood, 'This bow's no use at all.'

Robin stood ready at the line, and took an arrow out,
and shot six inches from the mark, no shadow of a doubt.
They all lined up and shot again, the Sheriff's men and he;
only the potter hit the mark; he split the stake in three.

The Sheriff's men were full of shame; the potter full of pride;
the Sheriff had to laugh it off, although he cringed inside:
'You see the skill this potter's got, to bend a bow or throw a pot!'
'I'm not bad with a decent bow,' the potter said. 'Mine's good.
The one I keep upon my cart, I got from Robin Hood.'

'From Robin Hood? Clearly, good potter, you are joking me!'
'No; many times I've shot with Robin, underneath the tree.'
'A hundred pounds,' the Sheriff swore, 'I'd freely give to see
that thief and liar here with me!'

'So come with me tomorrow,' said the potter, 'to the wood:
before you've had your breakfast, you'll have met with Robin Hood.'
'If I catch him,' the Sheriff said, 'then richly you'll be paid!'
The tournament was over then, and supper it was laid.

THE SHERIFF PAYS THE POTTER

No sooner did the sun rise than the Sheriff went to ride;
the potter harnessed up the cart, to drive along beside.
He said goodbye to the Sheriff's wife, with thanks for each good thing,
and left her with a souvenir, a little golden ring;
which made her eyes to glitter so, the Sheriff thought it odd;
'Let's get this potter on his way, without delay, by God!'

And when they came into the wood, under the leaves so green,
the little birds sang on the branch, so lovely to be seen.
'How lucky,' said the potter, 'it would be to live out here.
But never mind. We'd best find out if Robin Hood is near.'

He brought his horn up to his mouth, and blew it through and through;
and Robin's men, who heard it then, their master's music knew;
and through the trees, liked crazed men, faster than foxes flew.

And when they came to Robin Hood, then up spoke Little John:
'How did things go in Nottingham? How has your trading gone?'
'Well, mustn't grumble,' Robin said, 'such bargains as I've had.
I got a Sheriff for five pots – I'd say that wasn't bad.'

'*This* is the Sheriff here?' John said. 'Well, he's a sight to see.'
How eager was the Sheriff then back at his house to be!
'If I'd known you were Robin Hood, just this time yesterday,
then – potter – out of Nottingham you'd not have found a way!'

'And don't I know it,' Robin said, 'but now, thank God, we're here.
Now, Sheriff, leave your horse with us, and all your other gear.'
'Since so I must,' the Sheriff said, 'the loss good God beshrew!'
'You came on horseback,' Robin said; 'so walk home on your shoes,
and give my greetings to that wife you do such credit to.

'Give her this good white palfrey horse that ambles soft as dew;
and – lest I disoblige her – I shall do no worse with you.'
With that the Sheriff turned for home, and went his weary way;
his smart new wife welcomed him back – here's what she had to say:

'How has the forest-hunting gone? Did you catch Robin Hood?'
'Black Satan take him, blood and bone! I only wish I could.
'Each bit of gear I took from here, he's taken from my hands –
except, of course, for this white horse – that's yours, by his command.'

The Sheriff's wife laughed long and hard: 'Now, by God's Trinity,
you've paid him well for those five pots that he gave me for free.
But still – you're home – and safe and sound,
so welcome home from me!'
And Robin hailed the potter, underneath the green oak-tree:

'Potter, how much were those pots worth, that I went off to sell?'
'About ten pounds,' the potter said, 'just over, truth to tell;
since that's what I'd have got for them, if I'd been there myself.'

'Here's twenty times that,' Robin said; 'the joke's worth more to me;
and if you come this way again, let's have a drink or three!'
And, with that said, each went his way, under the green oak-tree.

And God save gracious Robin Hood, and keep the people free!

THE GEST OF ROBIN HOOD

THE POOR KNIGHT

When Robert Hood of Loxley was outlawed – as people had often said he would be, and they were sad as they said it, for Robin was a good lad, well liked in Loxley for his blue eyes and his winning ways, and an outlaw's life was generally hard and short – he fled at once to the wastes of Barnsdale. His parting shot was to say that he would obey the king's law when the king himself came to Barnsdale to enforce it, instead of leaving it to the sheriffs. Until then, he would feel safer in the forest than he ever did in the valley where he had grown up.

'In any case,' he would add, crossing himself with mock-seriousness, 'Our Lady Mary is there to protect me. And Mary will look after me, all right. If the stories the priests and friars tell are all true, Mary knows what it is to be an exile on the road, with a king in pursuit, with murder in his heart and an army at his back. Ave Maria, Lady of Thieves!'

Many in Loxley thought this was no more than one of Robin's jokes, but he was not smiling as he said it.

So Robin Hood began his career as an outlaw, and sure enough he was soon famous for his luck. He was said to be living at his ease in the forest, hunting, robbing travellers along the Great North Road – with or without the help of the Virgin Mary. He soon drew a band of kindred spirits around him. They wore

Robin's colours of green and scarlet, and their names are now famous: Little John, and Much the Miller's Son, and Will Scarlock. If anyone mentioned the king to Robin in those days, Robin would say that if the king ever came to Barnsdale, he had better come wearing green and scarlet, so as not to offend the locals.

This, seemingly, was another one of his jokes.

Once, Robin sent Little John, with Will Scarlock and Much the Miller's Son, to watch the Great North Road from Barnsdale Forest.

'Bring us a guest in to supper,' Robin said. 'See what their appetite's like, once we've told them who we really are.'

'A guest,' John smiled. 'Right.'

'A rich guest. An earl or an abbot.'

'Right,' John said again. 'We'll bring him. And after supper,' he added, 'you can tell him all about the Virgin Mary.'

He took his bow and quiver and beckoned to Will and Much.

In the gathering dusk, from the shadows of the trees, the three thieves watched the road as it wound down the wooded escarpment towards the boggy bed of the valley of Brockadale. Before long they saw a lone knight picking his way down the hill, hurrying against the gathering chill of evening. As he approached they saw that he was an odd sort of knight. His thinning hair was dishevelled, and his clothes and gear were patched and ragged. There were poor knights on the roads, but they were few and far between; most knights were rich men. With his rusty armour and starved-looking horse, this one seemed little more than a beggar.

'Still, he's got his own armour, so he's a knight, and he'll have to do,' John muttered.

He stepped into the road.

'Stop, friend,' he called to the knight, 'and come to supper with Robin Hood.'

The knight's eyes flickered cautiously towards the roadside.

'Supper? With Robin Hood?' he said.

There was no hiding it: the poor knight was being robbed, and he knew it. He yielded to superior force and followed the thieves quietly.

Deep in the forest, the thieves led the knight by the bridle towards the spreading shade of an ancient oak tree. From the boughs of the oak hung the bodies of the king's foresters and the Sheriff's men: those who had paid the price for trying to bring Robin Hood to book.

No sooner had the poor knight and his captors arrived, than out of the shadows, with barely the rustle of a leaf, dozens of thieves gathered, in their green and scarlet. Among them was a master thief with striking blue eyes glittering in the dark. 'Welcome stranger,' he said, 'to Saint Mary's chapel.'

'Saint Mary's chapel?' the knight muttered, glancing around and up at the dead men hanging between the leaves. 'Ave Maria! It's a privilege to meet you, master Robin Hood.'

And there under the oak tree the thieves spread a white cloth and served the stranger a supper, just as sociably as if they had all been in some rich man's home, for that was their custom. The knight was nonplussed, but he had no choice but to eat what was set before him, with as good a grace as he could muster. He saw the outlaws smiling grimly, and refused to glance up again at the bodies hanging from the oak tree. He ate and drank and talked, and then patted his mouth and stood up.

'Well,' he said, as calmly as he could, 'I really must be going, gentlemen. I shall be sure to stand you all a supper,' he added, 'should I happen to pass this way again.'

'You may never come this way again,' Robin Hood said pointedly. His hand went to his knife. 'So you had best settle the bill now.'

'Oh, the bill? Me settle the bill? So that's how it is,' the knight sighed, with a glance at the glitter of the thieves' knives. 'Well, friends … if it's my money that concerns you, I'll save you the worry.'

And the knight tipped his bags on to the ground. No river of gold came flowing out. When the bags hung empty in the knight's hands, scarcely ten shillings lay on the ground.

'There's your bill. Forgive me if I don't leave a tip,' the knight said.

'Where's the rest of it?' Robin demanded.

'There is no rest of it. That's all there is,' the knight said.

'How come?'

'I have been robbed already, by worse villains than you, my thieving friends – no offence. I have been fleeced by monks.'

'Stop talking in riddles, and tell me the whole story,' Robin said. His hand remained on the hilt of his knife, and his eyes still glittered.

'If you want the whole story, you had best begin by learning my name: Richard,' said the knight. 'Sir Richard of the Lee, and I have a son. He's twenty. A year ago, he was fighting at his first tournament, and his hand slipped. Knifed a man to death. There was a fine to pay, and it wasn't a small one, as you may imagine, for a man's life. The fine was more than my son, or I, could afford to pay. So I had to borrow money. And borrow I did, from the abbot of Saint Mary's Abbey, York.'

The whole company of thieves stirred and muttered, and glanced at Robin. The knight glanced around and swallowed his surprise.

'Saint Mary's Abbey?' Robin murmured. The knight had let slip the holy name, the one thing Robin truly revered. There was a thick silence among the thieves, as the thieves hung on Robin's words.

The knight had no choice but to forge ahead with his story.

'So instead of worrying about the fine, now I worry about the loan,' he went on. 'All year I have been saving. No luck. No money. No hope of going to London to pay for lawyers, or appeal to the king. The fine's all paid, anyway, and my boy's gone across the sea now, fighting strangers, and I hear he's doing pretty well. But I'm not. The debt to the abbot falls due tomorrow, and still I've scarcely a penny to my name. Well,' he sighed, 'so it must be. The monks will take every acre of the land that my fathers left me: the castle of the Lee, and Weardale besides. And when they have taken it,' the knight added, in a steady voice, 'I will take ship, and follow my boy, and go to Palestine, and die, and perhaps I will get more mercy from God in heaven, than ever I got from Saint Mary's monks on earth.'

He fell silent, and stared gloomily at the fire.

'Did you have no friend, willing to help?' Robin asked quietly.

'Friends?' The knight gave a hollow laugh. 'A poor man with friends?' Robin's hand was still on the haft of his knife.

'I'm lending you the money myself,' he said drily. 'Those monks have dishonoured the Virgin. They have slandered the name of

Our Lady of Thieves. So, Sir Richard, have the money. Have it from me, in Mary's name. Pay it me back when you can. We'll set a payment-day a year from now.'

Sir Richard glanced warily from outlaw to outlaw in the firelight. Nobody seemed to be smiling.

'Dishonoured the Virgin? Lend me the money? Are you joking?' Sir Richard asked frankly.

'I never joke,' Robin growled. 'Not about the holy Virgin.'

And he meant it. After supper was cleared away, deep in the shadows of the forest, Little John broke open a hollow tree and opened the secret hoard, counted out the glittering money into Sir Richard's saddlebags: four hundred pounds of gold. The thieves gave Sir Richard a suit of green and scarlet besides, and invited him to sleep over in the forest.

And so the evening ended, and the thieves melted away in the shadows, but Sir Richard knew that he would be watched, so he wrapped himself in his cloak and slept as best he could, under the hanging dead men, by the embers of the thieves' fire, in the place they called Saint Mary's chapel. Somehow he managed to sleep a little.

When he woke, he was alone. The birds were singing and the leaves were weaving the sunlight and the morning breeze. His horse was cropping the patchy forest turf contentedly and the embers were cold. He was alone, but his saddlebags were still stuffed with gold.

Sir Richard scratched his head. *Well*, he thought. *Evidently, I no longer need to worry about owing money to monks. I need to worry about owing money to thieves. Doesn't feel much different, really. Still, I have another year to find the money. That's progress of a sort.*

He sighed, and stretched.

'All I need to do now is find my way back to the road,' he muttered aloud.

'Don't worry for that,' came a deep, familiar voice. 'I'm coming with you to York.'

Sir Richard started, and turned to see the bulky form of Little John, stepping silently out of the shadowy forest.

'You can't go wandering around the forest with that kind of money,' John explained bluntly. 'There's thieves about.'

It was always hard to tell whether such things were meant as jokes.

'Besides,' John added, as if to himself, 'if I'm going to get preached at with the Virgin Mary, all day every day, I might as well go to the monks and get it done properly, in a bit of comfort. Robin can do without me for a season or two.' He caught the knight's expression, and added, 'Don't worry, Sir Richard: there is no catch. This is no trick. You will not be robbed – or not by me, at any rate. Robin Hood wants you to have the money and pay back the abbot. He trusts the Virgin Mary. And it seems he trusts you. I'll make sure you get safely to York. After that, we go our own ways.'

'Then you have my word,' Sir Richard replied, 'that the money will be repaid. On time. To Robin Hood.'

John would not answer, and the two men made their way to York in silence.

AT SAINT MARY'S ABBEY

The following night, in the flickering candlelight under the vast gilded canopy of the guildhall in York, Sir Richard of the Lee knelt before the abbot, and took off his cap and bowed respectfully.

Then he asked for more time to pay.

Robin's money already hung heavy at his waist in a bag, but the abbot knew nothing of it. Sir Richard was curious to hear what the abbot's answer would be. I'm going to enjoy this, Sir Richard was thinking.

The monks knew nothing of this; they sat before their steaming dinner plates and watched in utter silence. The feast had been at its noisy height only a moment before, but every monk in the hall knew the abbot wanted Sir Richard's castle and lands in Weardale, more than he wanted to go to heaven when he died, and they, too, wanted to see how this encounter would turn out.

In the silence, the Sheriff of Nottingham, the abbot's guest of honour, watched with amused detachment. He had no suspicion that Little John himself was in the streets outside, idly killing time with his own guards as they practised their archery.

The abbot waved a hand dismissively.

'No,' he told the knight, simply and flatly. 'There will be no more time to pay. That was not the agreement. The agreement was: cash or castle,' he said. 'Tonight. Now.'

'Then let it be cash,' Sir Richard said.

There was a gasp of surprise as Sir Richard rose stiffly to his feet, and tugged at his rags. They fell from him. Under his rags the knight wore green and scarlet: Robin Hood's livery. Suddenly, in the flickering candlelight, the knight suddenly looked like a wild thief from the forest.

And then Sir Richard upended the saddlebag. In the silence the gold coins almost seemed to roar, as they cascaded on to the floor-boards, and rang and rattled as they rolled under the tables and between the feet of the astonished monks. Sir Richard of the Lee threw the empty saddlebag down on the heap of coins and strode from the hall.

I was right, he thought as he went. *I did enjoy that.*

The abbot had not enjoyed it so much, but the good humour of the feast was soon restored, and the abbot made a point of laughing shrilly at every joke, and sending the wine round again.

It was some hours before the Sheriff of Nottingham finally left the feast, with a skinful of wine. He was intrigued to find a huge, cloaked stranger, a forester by the look of him, trading archery-shots with his guards in the streets. He did not approve of the men fraternising with commoners, and curtly asked the stranger his name and his business.

Little John was a practised and fluent liar.

'My name is Reynold Greenleaf,' John said. 'My business is forestry, but,' he went on, as an interesting possibility suddenly occurred to him, 'my master appears to have gone mad with religion. To be honest, sir, that can get on a man's nerves. Are you looking to hire servants? I can handle a bow, and turn my hand to anything, more or less. As long as nobody mentions the Virgin Mary. If you please, sir.'

Little John tugged his forelock. *Maybe that's a bit much*, he thought. *But the man's drunk. I'm safe.*

'Who is your master?' slurred the Sheriff, intrigued, and failing to spot the sarcasm.

'Sir Richard of the Lee,' lied Little John again.

'Sir Richard of the Lee? I've just seen him. You're quite right, the man's taken leave of his senses. Made a fool of the abbot in front of his own monks. The abbot will make him pay for that. But that's their business. So, Reynold Greenleaf,' the Sheriff slurred, 'why don't you come and work for me instead?'

It certainly amused the Sheriff to think he would be stealing such a good servant from the old knight, and he quickly settled terms with the huge man, and left for Nottingham.

Meanwhile, the monks of Saint Mary's slept in late on account of last night's feast, and, late next morning, before he rose for the day, the abbot summoned the high cellarer to his shuttered bedchamber.

'That old knight Sir Richard got off the hook somehow this year. But we'll get him next year. Don't worry. Let us be patient,' he said. 'Do nothing for a year. When the year comes round, take some money – twice the money – and ride to London. It's worth it for a castle like that. A good lawyer will tell any old lie if you pay him. Somehow we'll cook up some charge against Sir Richard, and get him exiled. And once he's exiled, with his lands confiscated and forfeit, we'll get his castle and his lands. And you can have his wife. If you want her. Now go. And shut the door quietly on your way out. I've got a headache.'

IN SERVICE WITH THE SHERIFF

And that was why Little John did not return to the forest. All that year, Robin missed him greatly, but he made no show of his feelings. Little John, meanwhile, remained in service with the Sheriff, still calling himself Reynold Greenleaf.

John knew that sooner or later he would return to the forest, but he was in no particular hurry. All that year, he served the Sheriff as he felt the Sheriff deserved – that is, badly. Months passed. Then, one morning, John slept in late, ignoring the Sheriff's summons for an early start, and the Sheriff waited and waited, and finally went hunting without him. Once they were all gone, John rose, scratched himself, and went for a late breakfast. The cook refused to serve him.

Suddenly, Little John realised that he had had enough. He was not cut out for the servant's life, and it was time to return to the forest. However, he thought he might as well go in style, so he punched the cook's head vigorously, and helped himself to breakfast. The cook was a hard-headed man, and regained consciousness in only a few moments.

'By God, that's a fist you've got there, Reynold Greenleaf.'

'Are you getting up?' John demanded, with his mouth full. 'You can always have some more, you know.'

'No,' the cook called out, prudently, from the floor where he lay. 'I think I'll just lie here for a moment. It's comfortable. Look, no hard feelings. Have a beer. Never too early for a beer. Barrel on your left. Best Christmas ale, on the house.'

'Thanks,' John agreed. 'That's neighbourly. Here, let me set you one up too. I hate to drink alone. No, don't sit up, I'll hand it down to you.'

The two men savoured their beer, and, having made each other's acquaintance in this rough and ready way, quickly found that they could get along well enough with a drink inside them. When the cook learned who he was really dealing with, he was suddenly stricken with admiration. He pictured himself telling the tale to his grandchildren: he once got his head punched by Little John himself. He glanced slyly at the huge man.

'How do you get to be an outlaw, then?' he asked.

'You know,' John replied flatly, with his mouth full. He waved a hand vaguely. 'Stealing things. Killing people.'

A look of greedy excitement flickered across the cook's fat face. John failed to notice it.

'Stealing things like the Sheriff's silver?' the cook asked slyly.

John belched, and nodded distractedly.

'That sort of thing,' he said, 'yes.'

'I've been working here a long time,' the cook said, with a slow wink. 'I know my way around. And the Sheriff's hunting in the forest all day.'

John's chewing ceased abruptly, and he looked up and noticed the tail-end of the wink.

'Feel free to stand up now,' he said. 'And take me to this silver.'

The cook was as good as his word, and they were two big men, more than a match for the bolts and bars on the Sheriff's treasury door, which they left in splinters.

And so it was that later that day, as the sun set in Barnsdale Forest miles away, Little John finally strode back into Robin's woodland hideout, his chapel of Saint Mary. Suddenly it was as if he had never been away, except that the cook was puffing along behind him, with a small fortune in silver in sacks between them, stolen from the Sheriff's treasury.

Robin glared at them.

'Where have you been?' Robin demanded.

'Oh, here and there,' John said. 'Sheriff's treasury. Sheriff's kitchen. All sorts of places. Warm places, with fires and ovens. It's been great. Nobody mentioned the Virgin Mary.'

'Well, it was nice of you to think of us,' Robin said.

'Wait,' said John, 'I've just had an idea. The Sheriff's hunting in the forest all day. Here, have this,' he said, beckoning to the cook and throwing down the sacks of silver. 'For starters.'

The silver clattered down on the turf beneath the gallows-oak, and Little John vanished into the forest, leaving the fat cook to give his own account of himself to the thieves.

John knew the Sheriff would be hunting somewhere nearby, and tracked him down easily enough, for the Sheriff had poor woodcraft.

Little John ran forward to him, and knelt on the earth with his usual show of humility.

'Reynold Greenleaf!' the Sheriff growled. 'Where were you when I wanted you this morning?'

'Forgive me, sir. I have been out scouting,' Little John answered humbly. 'And I have found a marvellous beast,' he added, his eyes wide with wonder. 'A stag like you've never seen. It's green and scarlet. But you must come alone.'

'A stag? Green? And *scarlet*?'

The Sheriff stroked his beard and gazed shrewdly at the big man. It occurred to him that it would be interesting to find out what his strange servant really meant.

He found out soon enough; before long he was standing captive under the swaying corpses of the gallows-oak, before the green-and scarlet-clad figure of Robin Hood.

'Told you,' Little John growled.

'Welcome to Saint Mary's chapel, Sheriff,' Robin said. His mood was lightening. 'Stay with us awhile, and see how you like it.'

The Sheriff had known some of the men who hung now between the oak-leaves; they were the very men he had sent into the forest himself, to hunt thieves. Little enough had he cared when they never came back, and small charity he had given to their widows. Alone as he was now, under their swaying feet, he bit his lip with apprehension. He practically bit his lip clean off with apprehension when Robin sounded his horn, and the thieves set a supper before him on his own silver, prepared by his own cook.

The thieves watched as he forced down a few mouthfuls.

'I can see you feel almost at home already,' Robin chuckled. 'Here. Let me take that richly furred robe. It will prove nothing but a hindrance in your new, active outdoor life. Sleep in your shirt. It's more wholesome, we find.'

If the Sheriff had made a sorry sight at supper, in the morning after his night under the swaying gallows-oak, he looked sorrier still: like a haunted man. He looked no happier when Robin told him that he had made such a good thief that they were minded to retain him on a permanent basis. At that the wretched Sheriff's nerve finally broke, and he swore an oath by the holy Virgin that he would leave all thieves and outlaws in peace until the year's end, if only they would let him go with his life.

Robin was not a man to lightly dismiss an oath to the Virgin, even from a man like the Sheriff. He reckoned the long-term odds, made the bargain, and let the Sheriff go. And that was why there was a truce between the outlaws and the Sheriff's men for the rest of the year.

They sent the Sheriff back to the road, and then sat down to talk.

'Once the Sheriff gets home,' John sighed, 'he'll be after us. He'll likely keep his word for the year, at most. We'll need money for hardware – arrows and knives, and the odd bribe. We could do with that four hundred.'

'What four hundred?' Robin asked.

'What four hundred? You're a fool, Robin Hood. The four hundred you lent to the knight a year ago. Sir Richard. I took him to York, remember. He owes you. The day's nearly due.'

'Oh, that four hundred. Don't worry, we'll get it.' Robin waved a hand. 'Sir Richard will pay the money if he's got it. And if he hasn't,' he added defiantly, 'there's always Our Lady of Thieves. The Virgin Mary herself has gone surety for the loan. Have some faith, John. Let the money come from men, or from miracles. It doesn't matter. It will come.'

'Oh God, not the Virgin Mary again,' John muttered wearily.

A LOAN REPAID

Meanwhile, all that year, at home in the castle of the Lee, Sir Richard had been saving his money.

A year later to the very day – just as the Sheriff was limping home from the forest, having sworn an oath of peace with the outlaws – Sir Richard set off for Barnsdale again, with four hundred pounds in a new saddlebag, to repay the loan to the thieves and put an end to the whole matter.

In the afternoon, he came to the village of Wentbridge, at the edge of Brockadale.

At Wentbridge, the village green was all astir. There was a prize-fight on, the kind of fight that made Wentbridge famous. A trestle had been set up by the green, and a fat-looking wine barrel had been set up and tapped, ready to broach and drink. The fight was between all comers, with the wine as prize. The sport had lasted all day, and taken a grim turn, and half a dozen villagers had broken the rules, joined in the fight, and were pummelling a poor blacksmith to within an inch of his life; he had been a strong man when he had begun fighting that morning, but now he was nothing but a bed of bruises. A bloodthirsty crowd was ringing the boxers round as they fought, and the air was full of shouting and swearing as the fight swayed to and fro about the green.

Sir Richard took it all in at a glance, and, being something of a sportsman himself, he took a dislike to what he saw.

'What's afoot here?' demanded Sir Richard, raising his voice.

'Barrel of wine for the winner, sir,' came the explanation.

The man who had answered pointed briefly at the trestle with the fat barrel on it.

'Never mind that. Six on to one?' Sir Richard shouted. 'What sort of odds is that? It won't do.'

He drew his sword and spurred his horse into the throng.

The commotion suddenly ceased. The people of Wentbridge knew better than to face a fully armed man in his anger.

'You, blacksmith,' the knight called, pointing his sword at the battered and gasping blacksmith. 'I am Sir Richard of the Lee, knight of this county, and I hereby declare *you*, sir, the winner. The wine's yours. Now, let me offer you five pounds in exchange for it. Do we have a bargain? Yes? Thank you. Good. So now, gentlemen, the wine is *mine*. And as a token of my esteem I wish to present it – the whole barrel of it – to the people of Wentbridge, to share equally, fair and square.

'So now, gentlemen, the wine belongs to *you*. To *us*. All of us. Someone pour me a half of it. And let's have no more of this thuggery. Six on one, indeed. It's a disgrace. I thought Wentbridge was a better place than that.'

So impressed were the people of Wentbridge with the knight's plain but generous dealings that they would not let Sir Richard go without taking another half-pint, and then another. As a knight and a sportsman, Sir Richard could hardly refuse. So there was singing, and dancing, and evening drew on with its chilly mists, with the revels showing no sign of abatement. Sir Richard now had little option but to throw himself into the revelry – and, besides, it is pleasant to be toasted as a hero by an entire village, particularly one as famous as Wentbridge for its tough customers.

But miles away, through the shadowy forests of Barnsdale, Robin Hood was waiting, hungry and impatient, to see if he would get his four hundred-pound loan repaid, whether by the hand of man or the miracle of the Virgin.

That evening, the shadows lengthened over the cooling earth. Still Sir Richard did not appear.

Robin grew gloomy, and began kicking pebbles impatiently around the camp.

'Go up Brockadale and see if he's coming,' he told Little John. 'Because, if he isn't,' he added vengefully, 'you won't want to miss the miracle.'

John sighed, and set off with Will and Much to watch the Great Road again.

They went, and watched, and saw no sign of Sir Richard.

'That's it,' John grumbled. 'Sir Richard's not coming, and the money's gone. Bloody religion. I told Robin I wanted no more of it, and when I –'

But then, before the thieves' very eyes, the miracle was beginning.

For down the steep hill towards the river, the thieves saw, not a knight, but a fat-headed monk, riding from York: a monk of Saint Mary's Abbey.

It chanced, you see, to be the very day that the high cellarer of Saint Mary's Abbey was heading to London with secret bribes for the lawyers, to cook up some charges against Sir Richard in the hopes of finally getting hold of his castle. After a long year's waiting, the abbot's plan was coming to fruition. But the outlaws on the roads, Much and Will, knew nothing of this. They saw a monk of Saint Mary herself, Our Lady of Thieves, on the Virgin's own payment-day, riding towards them, unprepared for highway robbery.

'Stop, friend! Stand and deliver!'

'Stop?' the monk sneered. 'For whom? Robin Hood?'

The struggle which followed was brief and conclusive, and the outlaws carried the monk away into the forest, and Robin himself was waiting for them in the shadows under the gallows oak, his eyes glittering in the dusk.

When the thieves pulled the bag off the monk's fat head, he just glared.

'No use wasting courtesy on monks,' Little John observed. 'You get none back.'

'The high cellarer of Saint Mary's Abbey,' said the fat-headed monk, 'squanders no courtesies on thieves and outlaws.'

Robin started.

'Saint Mary's Abbey!' he exclaimed. 'It's a sign! Saint Mary's Abbey! Thanks be to God! This man has brought us that four hundred, John. Told you.'

John gazed doubtfully at the fat monk.

'You wait and see. It's a miracle. Sir Richard has been delayed by God's hand, to test our faith. And this miracle has come to us instead, to strengthen our faith in his holy mother.

'Still, first things first. Let's have supper, like always. Then we'll see what our friend has got in his pockets.'

Theological disputations were set aside for a moment, then, and the feast was set on the earth as it always was, under the creaking ropes and swaying shoes of the gallows-oak, as the thieves' habit was.

The monk, like the knight before him, had no choice but to eat what was set before him. He managed to force a few mouthfuls past the dryness of his throat. It was not the way he was accustomed to take his supper, and the meal was soon over.

'So, cellarer,' Robin said, calmly. 'Has the Virgin Mary sent you to me? Have you brought me my four hundred?'

'The Devil has driven you mad,' the high cellarer muttered, and John looked as if he might agree.

'We shall see how mad the Devil has driven me,' Robin said. He drew his glittering knife. 'How much is there in your saddlebags and coffers, would you say?'

The high cellarer's manner changed quite promptly. 'Maybe eight pounds?' he lied, desperately. 'For travel expenses,' he explained.

'Eight pounds? Well, I shall not rob you of eight pounds. Our Lady promised me four hundred. If there is no more than eight pounds in those coffers of yours, you shall be returned to the road, unrobbed and unmolested.'

And, with that, Little John broke into the coffers.

The secret bribes for the London lawyers flooded out onto the outspread cloth, with a gluttonous roar of cascading gold coins.

It was Robin who broke the silence.

'Ave Maria!' he cried. 'A miracle! Our Lady of Thieves has repaid the loan!'

It was a special moment for them all. All the thieves saw was the miracle. Even John muttered a short prayer. As for the others, their master, Robin Hood, they thought, must be a prophet of God himself. The thieves and exiles all fell to their knees at once to offer a prayer of thanks.

Naturally, however, no prayer was as fervent as the fat-headed monk's.

The heap of coins, once counted, made well over the four hundred pounds. The thieves took the money, and let the fat monk ride off, glad to escape with his life, happy to have paid for his supper with no more than his secret stash of bribe money. And when the thieves had waved the fat-headed monk off to London, and turned to go back to the forest, they heard the sound of marching feet, and rough singing, coming down from the north on the other side of the valley.

And they looked out against the sunset, and who did they see there but Sir Richard of the Lee rolling down the forest road, weary with revelry and wrestling and half-drunk from sharing his barrel of wine.

They welcomed him in, and made a second feast, and a much more cheerful one. For Sir Richard had brought the four hundred pounds which he had been saving, so between his money and the monks', the knight and the thieves were repaid several times over. Robin Hood and Sir Richard drank many healths to the holy Virgin under the gallows-oak, and parted in friendship, and went their ways unmolested, thanks to the Sheriff's reluctant oath.

'See?' Robin said to John, as they waved Sir Richard off. 'We are rich men again, and free, and we have a year of peace. Doesn't Saint Mary the Virgin always looks after her thieves?'

But the year of the Sheriff's oath was soon over. And in all Nottingham and the villages round Barnsdale Forest, as far north as Blyth and Doncaster, nobody was fool enough to think that the Sheriff would not seek revenge against Robin Hood, once the terms of his oath permitted him. The year ended quietly.

THE SILVER ARROW

The next year began with the offer of a tempting prize: a silver arrow, fletched with feathers of gold. It was to be awarded by the Sheriff at an archery contest in Nottingham, on a certain day in the New Year. The day came round, and Robin set seven score men around him, and made his way to Nottingham. Little John shot well that day, and Will Scarlock and Much the Miller's Son, but Robin Hood split the stake in three straight bouts, and won the silver arrow. Robin mounted the grandstand with a winning smile, and the crowd's applause ringing in his ears, to take the arrow from the Sheriff's gloved hand. But he saw from the Sheriff's smile, and the shrewd look in his eyes as he handed over the arrow, that he was known and discovered. And as they left the throng about the archery butts on the green, the Sheriff gave a signal, and the horns rang, and the Sheriff's trap was sprung.

And it was no soft trap that Robin Hood was caught in, for there on the town walls, and in the crowd, and in the streets between the green and the town gates, were a dozen of the Sheriff's men for every one of the thieves; black-coated, hard-faced, armoured head to foot. Their swords and knives glittered cruelly in the afternoon sun.

Robin let the silver arrow fall, and reached for his sword.

There was a running battle fought in the very streets of Nottingham that day. The thieves might have won to freedom, but, just as they reached the very gates, an arrow struck Little John in the back of the knee, and giant as he was, he fell hard.

Robin leaned over Little John where he lay, and his face was pale. 'Kill me. Don't let them take me alive,' John rasped.

Robin nodded, and said nothing, but heaved his friend's full weight up on his shoulders, and carried him.

They made the gates together, and ran into the hills, hardly knowing or caring where they ran. And at the end of that weary day, pursued by the Sheriff's men, the thieves sought sanctuary at a little castle in a valley nearby, and when the lord came to speak with them, Robin found himself gazing into the astonished face of his old friend Sir Richard. The thieves were soon safe within the walls, and the walls themselves were soon clustered thick with Sir Richard's men, with longbows and arrows hungry for a bite of the flesh of the Sheriff's men. Outside the castle, the Sheriff's men beat fruitlessly at the studded gates, and sounded their horns, and sent word to Nottingham that Robin Hood, the master thief, had been run to ground at the castle of the Lee in Weardale. All that year, Nottingham had been looking for trouble, and now, at last, it had come.

THE SIEGE OF WEARDALE

The Sheriff came himself with every black-coated thug he could hire. The abbot of Saint Mary's Abbey in York paid for mercenaries from Cheshire and Derbyshire, and it was no small army that laid siege to Sir Richard's little castle. Day and night men in black coats and gleaming armour clustered thick on the forecourt, and there were taunts and jeers back and forth over the wall as those within grew weak with hunger and fear.

'The king will hear of this!' the Sheriff yelled, shaking his fist at the distant figures on the castle walls.

And sure enough, within the week, the Sheriff's herald appeared before the gates under a flag of truce, and held up a letter under the royal seal. Sir Richard's porter brought the letter from the gates, and when Sir Richard read it, his face went white.

'The king is coming. To Nottingham. To hear the case for himself. Two weeks' truce he has ordered till he can come.'

'Does he mean it?'

'The king never jokes.'

'*I* never joke,' Robin said.

'That'll be another one of your jokes,' John said. 'This is King Edward we're dealing with. Don't think the Virgin Mary's going to bail us out this time, is she?'

There was a moment's silence.

'Well,' Sir Richard said, with a sigh. 'We have two weeks. Go back to the forest and keep good order there, as good as you can. Whatever the king does or doesn't do, or the Sheriff, we won't be much help to each other cooped up here like chickens.'

The next day, the thieves took their leave of Sir Richard and, slipping out at a postern, they returned to Barnsdale. There they set up camp again, in Saint Mary's chapel under the gallows-oak. They cut down the dead and buried the bodies decently at last in the earth, and it was good that they did, for ten days later, Sir Richard's wife sought them out in Barnsdale. Her face was pale and set, and she came to the point.

'Richard,' she said, 'is in chains in Nottingham. They're going to hang him.'

'Who's going to hang him? The king? Has the king come to Nottingham?' Robin demanded.

She clicked her tongue. 'Of course not. The Sheriff broke the truce. Richard trusted him to keep it, like a fool. Four days ago he went hunting. I told him not to go, but he laughed. He got caught, and it's taken me this long to find where he is, and find you to tell you about it.'

The thieves marched in massed ranks down the high road openly, like an army of green and scarlet, and wore no hoods or masks on their faces.

On the morning of the hanging, the mass of thieves passed through the town gates. The people fled before them, and they came to the town square. Sir Richard was there, with his head shaved and his hands bound, chained to a cart that was crawling towards a newly built gibbet, with a great crowd around it.

The Sheriff was supervising proceedings from a low balcony.

Over the crowded heads flew Robin Hood's arrow. It split the Sheriff's ribs. Down the Sheriff fell, and before he could rise, Robin ran up, and finished his work for the day. The Sheriff lay dead. The thieves, with Sir Richard among them, turned and ran for the town gates, scattering the terrified people as they went.

KING EDWARD'S DUTY

After two weeks, the king came.

His men came first. Suddenly Nottingham was full of them; the inns in every town were full of the armoured men who had burned Wales and France in King Edward's name.

The king's servants requisitioned the fugitive Sir Richard's castle in Weardale.

Pale servants and scarred, hard-faced men of war came and went around the king's secluded apartments in the castle, bringing news, and taking orders. Anyone who had ever met Robin Hood of Barnsdale was summoned to the king's rooms to tell what they knew. Few dared defy the summons, and it was hours before they emerged, their ears ringing with questions, and their tongues stilled by an oath of secrecy.

Little otherwise was ever seen of the king himself.

For weeks the king's servants hunted for Robin Hood, but could not find him.

The king's terror ruled road and town by day and night. Still Robin Hood eluded every trap.

In these dark days the thieves happened one evening to stop a band of travellers in monks' habits, a mile into Barnsdale on the road. Robin himself led the raid, and he was glad that he did, for these were no ordinary monks: the foremost among them wore the robe of an abbot. He stepped forward to take the abbot's bridle.

'Donations for the poor thieves of Saint Mary the Virgin!'

'To hell with Saint Mary the Virgin,' the abbot said dryly.

There was a shocked silence.

'But if you want to see my money, thief, there it is.'

Robin emptied the saddlebags with his own hands. Clearly this was no ordinary abbot. But he was no liar – forty pounds was indeed all he had.

'Forty pounds and not a penny more. If you mean to rob me of it, and face the consequences, then there it is. Take it,' the abbot said.

He threw his cloak aside, to show the image of the royal seal sewn on to his coat, and it seemed to Robin that at last he understood.

'The king's own clerks!' he said. 'When first I took to the roads I swore that I would obey the king's law if ever the king came to the forest. And it seems he is a man of his word, and he has sent his clerks ahead to put everything in order.'

'He has,' the abbot said. 'I bring a message from the king, to the one who calls himself Robin Hood. Is he here?'

'I will take you to him,' Robin said, and bowed low to honour the image of the king's seal.

The thieves led the monks into the trees. There in the shadows of the depths of the forest, under the oak where the frayed knots still hung, Robin turned.

'Sir monk, you came, so you say, with a message for Robin Hood. Well, I am Robin Hood, and before I hear your message, I will see what kind of men you are, you and your fellow-clerks.'

The abbot took a step back. He saw that the thieves' hands were reaching for arrows and bows, and he seemed to be preparing himself to fight.

But there was no bloodshed. The thieves were setting up archery targets on the butts; they had nothing worse in mind than a shooting match.

'Archery? Me? I am a man of God, thief, and I play no such games,' said the abbot.

'Don't you? We will see,' Robin said.

They set up garlands as targets, and agreed the prize: the loser to take a blow undefended from the winner, without flinching.

Robin shot, and split the stakes, one by one, and won against all comers, and one by one he punched them all to the ground with his fist; but when he shot against the abbot, he missed the mark by three fingers' breadth, and laid his bow aside.

'You win, abbot,' he said dryly. 'Now let me see if you can strike a blow.'

The abbot shook his head.

'I will strike no blow against you. I am a man of God, remember. And of peace.'

'You entered this contest with us, and a man of God cannot break his word,' Robin said.

'Then so be it, master thief,' said the abbot. 'Since you have reproved me, on my word I must put forth my full strength against you. And so I shall. Remember this when you bear the consequences.'

And he rolled up his sleeve, and flexed his arm.

'Strike as hard as you please,' said Robin defiantly.

And the abbot drew back his fist, and let it fly at the outlaw with all his strength, and the force of the blow lifted Robin Hood from the forest floor and sent him sprawling on the earth.

Robin Hood spat out some fragments of teeth.

'It is as I thought,' he lisped, rubbing his jaw. 'Whatever you are, king's clerk, you are no monk.'

'No monk, and no clerk,' the abbot said, and threw his cloak and hat aside. The image of the seal shone in gold thread on his coat as he drew out the long chain that hung round his neck; and there on the chain for the first time they all saw, not the image of the seal, but the seal itself: the great seal of England, that none could carry but the king.

Robin knelt with his face still bloody, and Sir Richard knelt, and the whole company of outlaws knelt again.

And then the king spoke.

'Robert Hood,' the king said. 'Long ago – so you say – you promised that you would heed the king's law when the king came to Barnsdale Forest to enforce it. And I have come. What do they call you now? Robin of Barnsdale, is it? Or Robin of Sherwood? Or Robin Hood? Names are no matter. Listen to me. I have burned France and I have burned Wales, and I have burned half of England because they defied me. I do not fear death. I do not fear hell. I do not fear God, or the holy Virgin Mary who fled from kings. They tell me that you were a good lad once, Robert – so I will be merciful. Surrender. If you surrender, I will pardon you freely and take you into my service. Defy me once more, and I will burn the North as my fathers burned it.'

Robert Hood of Loxley opened his mouth, and closed it, and opened it.

Finally, he bowed his head.

'My lord king,' he murmured.

The king smiled grimly, and nodded.

'Good lad,' the king said, with a smile. 'What must be must be. But let us at any rate,' he added, 'hear no more tales of Robin Hood.'

And Robert Hood of Loxley rode out from Barnsdale Forest at last, an outlaw no longer, but a common servant of the royal household.

And as they rode, by royal command, King Edward and all his men wore green and scarlet – for it amused the king to ride through the forest wearing the green and scarlet of the forest thieves. He would not wish to offend the locals, he explained, with a glance at Robin.

And that was how the king came to the forest, and Robin at last obeyed the law; and when the people saw them riding to Nottingham, they marvelled, for they could not tell which among the riders was the outlaw, and which was the king.

THE SOUNDING OF THE HORN

All that year Robin kept to the king's service in London, and he hardly touched a bow, and would not go to see a shooting match; but he kept his great horn silent beside him.

One day in London, he happened to walk past a window in the palace, and see a shooting match in the yard below among the king's men. He watched the singing leap of the arrow from the bow, and his hands remembered.

Robin went to the king, and asked leave to go for old times' sake to a chapel of Saint Mary's where he had been in the habit of saying his prayers.

And the king, not understanding his meaning, looked askance at him, and gave him leave, and told him he would be wanted at court again in seven days.

And Robin came to Barnsdale, and found the old chapel of Saint Mary under the ancient oak; and as the birds sang around him, he put his great horn to his lips, and sounded it again.

The sun shone on the restless leaves, and there was silence, and then Robin heard a deep, familiar voice, surprisingly close.

'You can't go wandering around Barnsdale making that kind of noise. There's thieves about.'

Robin turned to see the bulky form of Little John, stepping silently out of the shadowy forest. The big man had been living hard. He looked more like a bear than a man, or a monster carved in the walls or benches of a church. Much and Will were with him, and they looked worse. But when John smiled ruefully, it was the same old smile.

'I've had days,' he said, 'when I almost wished I could hear your preaching again.'

'My preaching days are over,' Robin replied.

'Suits me,' Little John said.

And so Robin Hood returned to Saint Mary's chapel, deep in the shadows of Barnsdale Forest, never to be seen again in the towns of England. And Little John was with him.

When the seven days were up, King Edward missed his famous servant. For a few days, he was troubled and angry, and considered sending searchers to the northern forests. But once his temper had had a chance to cool a little, he decided to wait, and see if time would bring news of any serious unrest in the North. Time passed, and no such news ever came, so, in the end, the king did nothing. Or nearly nothing: mainly for appearances' sake, he issued a proclamation to his officers, servants and loyal subjects, that they were to keep watch for the fugitive Robert Hood, and arrest him if he fell into their hands. But the fugitive Robert Hood failed to fall into anyone's hands, and the king did not pursue the matter. He let Robin Hood be.

And so, with a handful of friends by his side, all of them shrewd and quiet men, Robin Hood robbed the roads, and hunted the king's deer, through all the forests of South Yorkshire and beyond, until his death.

But his death is another story; and it happened in another county.

4

MONSTERS
AND MIRACLES

ST FRANCIS OF CONISBROUGH

The Naylor brothers (1916) record that:

> ... a curious old legend was attached to the town well in Wellgate, which formerly supplied most of the inhabitants of Conisborough with water; for once upon a time, when the town was suffering from a great drought, and the people feared a water famine, they consulted an old man known by the name of St Francis, who was very wise and very holy. He told the people to follow him, singing psalms and hymns to the Willow Vale, on the Low Road. There he cut a wand from a willow tree, and stuck it into the ground, and forthwith a copious supply of water appeared which had flowed steadily ever since. The wand had been so firmly and deeply stuck into the ground by St Francis that it took root and grew into a large tree.

The Holy Well still stands under a low stone shelter about halfway up Wellgate, in Conisbrough, running north-west from St Peter's church. Willow Vale lay a short walk to the south-east: it was a plantation along the banks of Kearsley Brook, a tributary of the Don, probably maintained for basket-making. Nowadays, Willow Street runs nearby.

The Holy Well, Conisbrough

The Naylors do not mention where the mysterious St Francis planted the willow; the nearby Holywell Lane appears to mark a similar but separate well, which was restored and rededicated in 2003.

THE DRAGON OF WANTLEY

The story of the Dragon of Wantley first appears in broadsides of the 1680s and was reprinted many times in the years following its first appearance. In 1737 it was used as the basis of a burlesque opera by Henry Carey, which was staged at the Haymarket Theatre and Covent Garden, London. Following a reference in passing in Walter Scott's Ivanhoe, in 1892, it was rewritten again as a novel by the US author Owen Wister, most famous for his novel The Virginian. The Naylor brothers in 1916 curiously state that the dragon-slayer was Guy of Warwick, rather than the more common More of More Hall.

Our text is taken (word for word) from a broadside entitled 'An Excellent Ballad of the most Dreadful Combat Fought Between Moore [sic] of Moore-hall, and the Dragon of Wantley' (Deacon 2002 (1983): 214–15). It was apparently printed in London in the decades around 1800 and preserved in Frederick Madden's collection, now housed in Cambridge University. We have preserved the punctuation of the original almost exactly.

Some scholars have long argued that the story of this particular dragon was a satire directed against a local landowning family. The Naylors in 1916 explained 'Wantley' as an old name for 'Wharncliffe'. The 'Dragon's Den' – a cave in the gritstone escarpment – is marked on OS maps of Wharncliffe Crags, north of Sheffield. The crags abut on Wharncliffe Chase, an ancient centre of settlement, quarrying and smelting, and a medieval hunting reserve which is still a popular local resort for rock-climbing and other pastimes. The topographical details in the ballad – the unbreakable stones, and the well containing the dragon's 'burning snivil' – seem to be knowing references to the landscape around Wharncliffe Crags.

On the opposite side of the valley, close to More Hall itself, Wantley Dragon Wood is a new plantation near Bitholmes Wood, complete with an evocative sculpture of the dragon, in wood and dry stone. An 1897 bas-relief sculpture of a dragon-slaying knight, in the lobby of Sheffield Town Hall, is usually said to be an illustration of the death of the Dragon of Wantley – although it differs in detail from the story. When the ballad calls the dragon's hide 'as tough / as any buff,' the reference seems to be to the toughened leather, or the hardwearing 'buff coats' made out of it, which were favoured particularly by soldiers.

Old stories tell how *Hercules*,
a dragon slew at *Lernia*,
with seven Heads and fourteen Eyes,
to see and well discern-a,
But he had a club,
This Dragon to drub,
or he had ne'er don't I warrant ye;
but moore of moore-hall,
With nothing at all,
he slew the Dragon of Wantley.
This Dragon had two furious Wings,
each one upon his Shoulder;
With a sting in his tail, as long as a flail,
which made him look bolder and bolder.
He had long Claws,
and in his Jaws
four and forty teeth of Iron;
With a hide as tough,
As any buff,
which did him round inviron.
Have you not heard of the Trojan horse
had seventy Men in his belly?
This Dragon was not quite so big,
but very near I tell ye:
Devour did he,
Poor Children three,
that could not with him grapple,
And at one sup
He ate them up,
as one should eat up an apple.
All sorts of cattle this dragon did eat,
some say he did eat up trees,
And that the forest sure he would
devour up by degrees:
For houses and churches,
Were to him geese and turkies:

eat all, and left none behind,
But some stones, dear Jack,
Which he could not crack,
which on the hills you will find.
In Yorkshire, near fair *Rotheram*,
the place I know it well,
Some two or three miles, or there abouts,
I vow I cannot tell;
But there is a hedge,
Just on the hill-edge,
and Matthew's house hard by it;
Oh! there and then,
Was this dragon's den,you could not chuse but spy it.
Some say, this Dragon was a witch,
some say, he was a devil,
For from his nose a smoke arose,
and with his burning snivil,
Which he cast off
When he did cough
in a well that he did stand by,
Which made it look,
Just like a brook
running with burning brandy.
Hard by a furious knight there dwelt,
of whom all towns did ring:
For he could wrestle, play at quarter-staff, kick, cuff and huff,
call son of a whore, do any kind of thing:
By the tail and the main,
With his hands twain,
he swung a horse till he was dead:
And what is stranger,
He for very anger
eat him all up but his head.
These children, as I told, being eat,
men, women, girls, and boys,
Sighing and sobbing, came to his lodging,

and made a hedious noise:
Oh, save us all,
Moore of moore-hall,
thou peerless knight of these woods!
Do but slay this dragon,
He won't leave us a rag on;
we'll give thee all our goods.
Tut, tut, quoth he, no goods I want,
but I want, I want in sooth,
A fair maid of sixteen, that's brisk,
and smiles about the mouth:
Hair as black as a sloe,
Both above and below,
with blushing cheeks adorning,
To 'noint me o're night,
E're I go to fight,
and to dress me in the morning.
This being done, he did engage
to hew this dragon down:
but first he went, new armour to
bespeak at *Sheffield* town;
With spikes all about,
Not within, but without,
of Steel so sharp and strong,
Both behind and before,
Arms, legs, all o're,
some five or six inches long,
Had you seen him in this dress,
how fierce he look'd, and how big,
You would have thought him for to be
an Egyptian Porcupig:
He frighted all,
Cats, dogs, and all,
each cow, each horse, and each hog,
For fear did flee
For they took him to be

some strange outlandish hedge-hog.
To see this fight all people then
got upon trees and houses,
On churches some, and chimneys too,
but they put on their trowzes,
Not to spoil their hose:
As soon as he rose,
to make him strong and mighty,
He drank, by the tale,
Six pots of ale,
and a quart of Aqua vitæ,
It is not strength that always wins,
for wit doth strength excel,
Which made our cunning champion
creep down into a Well
Where he did think,
This Dragon would drink,
and so he did in truth;
And as he stoop'd low,
He rose up and cry'd, boh,
and hit him in the mouth.
Oh, quoth the dragon, pox take you, come out,
thou that disturb'st my drink;
and then he turn'd and shit at him:
good lack, how he did stink!
Beshrew thy soul,
Thy body is foul,
thy dung smells not like balsam:
Thou son of a whore,
Thou stink'st so sore,
sure thy diet it is unwholesome.
Our politick knight on the other side,
crept out upon the brink,
And gave the Dragon such a douse
he knew not what to think:
By cock, quoth he;

Say you so, do you see?
and then at him he let fly
With hand and with Foot,
And so they went to't,
and the word it was hey, boys, hey,
Your words, quoth th'dragon, I don't understand.
Then to it they fell at all,
Like two boars so fierce, I may
compare great things with small;
Two days and a night,
With this Dragon did fight
our champion on this ground:
Tho' their strength it was great,
Yet their skill it was neat,
they never had one wound.
At length the hard earth began to quake,
the dragon gave him such a knock,
Which made him to reel, and straight he thought
to lift him as high as a rock,
And thence let him fall;
But Moore of Moore-hall
like a valiant son of Mars,
As he came like a lout,
So he turned him about,
and hit him a kick on the arse.
Oh, quoth the dragon with a sigh,
and turn'd six times together,
Sobbing and tearing, cursing and swearing,
out of his throat of leather:
Moore of Moore-hall,
Oh thou rascal! Would I had seen thee never,
With the thing at thy foot,
Thou hast prick'd my arse-gut;
oh, I am quite undone for ever.
Murder, murder, the Dragon cry'd,
alack, alack, for grief,

Had you but mist that place, you could
have done me no mischief:
Then his head he shak'd,
Trembled and quak'd,
and down he laid and cry'd;
First on one knee,
Then on back tumbl'd he,
so groan'd, kick'd, shit, and dy'd.

St William of Lindholme

No bride would marry in Thorne or Hatfield without going to visit William the Hermit. No girl ever looked forward to her visit. Saint he was called, but he seemed more witch than saint. He lived in a cave on the island of Lindholme, close to the heart of the sprawling fen of Hatfield Chase. There, just before the curtained-off cave mouth, so the story goes, ran a spring of fresh water, and sorrow and misfortune would always attend the bride who neglected to visit the old man and take a drink of the waters at his hands on her wedding day, with her bridegroom beside her as she drank. Who knows what old sorcery or charm flowed with the water, or its keeper, but people thought it best to respect the old custom.

There was once a girl in Thorne called Rosa. Her eye had been caught by a young gentleman's son, whose name was Walter Loveleigh. Rosa could hardly believe that Walter might love her in return. But he did, and, what was more, their parents seemed well disposed to the match – which mattered greatly in those days.

Rosa could not imagine ever being happier, and the happiest days of Walter's life were likewise his last few days of sweet freedom and carelessness, and even sweeter anticipation, before the betrothal was announced publicly, and the banns read. In an exalted mood, he was out hunting wildfowl on the marshy Chase, and happened to pass by Lindholme on his way home. There stood the low mound with the dark, curtained cave-mouth, and the strange white-watered spring bubbling forth. Walter, feeling like he was the king of the world, idly cut a turf and dammed the hermit's spring, the way a schoolboy might, just to see if the water would stop.

But the water did not stop. For a moment the channel ran dry and the water overflowed on to the springy turf by the reed margin.

Then the curtain sprang aside, and there in the cave-mouth stood the saint. The glare in the old man's pale eyes went right through Walter Loveleigh, and the banter he had been preparing died on his lips.

Walter smiled weakly. The saint kicked the turf out of the channel, and freed the water; and it ran back in the channel again.

The old man and the young hunter stood for a moment, staring at the spring.

'Set the cup to your lips, and you drain it to the lees,' the old man muttered, and he turned and disappeared behind the curtain.

Walter was left alone on the marsh. Slowly, he picked his way across it, back towards Thorne, in a rather shamefaced silence.

The betrothal was announced, and the banns read, and when the wedding was over, it was time for the couple to visit the hermit, and seek a drink for the bride from the holy well.

Walter had told Rosa nothing of his previous encounter. He wondering if the old man would remember him.

They rode out to Lindholme, and hailed the hermit in his cell, and the hermit showed no sign of recognition. He received them with a rough word of welcome. He dipped a stone cup in the water of the little channel, and held it out to Rosa.

Walter glanced anxiously down.

Seeing the young couple hesitate, the hermit said, 'Set the cup to your lips, and you drain it to the lees.'

Walter nearly spoke, but he could think of no words to say. He let Rosa drink.

Rosa drained the cup and handed it to the hermit with a smile. By the time the couple returned home, Rosa was already faint; she took to her bed at once, and never rose from it. She sickened and died a virgin bride.

It is said that the townsfolk, enraged by the death of the lovely Rosa, and loth to blame one of their own, ran to Lindholme to confront the hermit, and tore the curtain down. But the saint was lying in the cave, on his low bed, quite still and cold; he, too, had breathed his last. A cup of the spring-waters stood half-drunk by his pillow. It was as he had said: the hermit, like the bride and groom, had drained the bitter cup of life to the lees.

We learned the macabre story of William of Lindholme from W. Read (1858), as cited by F.H. Dallas (1995). Dallas could find no reference to a Loveleigh family of Thorne, or a St William of Lindholme. As Read tells the story, Rosa was indeed poisoned deliberately by the vengeful William, who then commits suicide. Given all this melodrama, it seems plausible to suggest that Read invented some or all of the story to suit the sensational tastes of popular readers of his own time. However, as so often, there seems to be a genuine tradition under all the elaboration. On the nearby Isle of Axholme, William of Lindholme was remembered as a giant and/or wizard, who performed several extraordinary feats by physical and/or satanic strength. He half-completed a causeway across Hatfield Chase, undertaking:

… to do it as fast as a man could gallop a horse, on condition that the rider should not look behind him. When the person had proceeded a few yards he heard such a noise and confusion that his fears got the better of his resolution; he looked back and saw … William in the midst of hundreds of little demons … The terrified horseman exclaimed, 'God speed your work,' which … put a stop to the whole business. (Quoted in Briggs 1991 (1970), Part B, Vol. 4: 394–95.)

This William also eventually committed suicide in his own cell – a point of similarity with the hermit-saint whose story we tell here. Maureen James, in Lincolnshire Folk Tales, *in the same series as the present volume, tells the story of the related wonder-working Tommy Lindum of Wroot. William seems quite a mythic figure – an odd overlap of giant, wizard, and earth-dwelling holy man with a vengeful streak.*

*The legend seems to derive from a prehistoric burial site. In 1727,
a Mr George Stovin wrote to the* Gentleman's Magazine *(Vol. XVII:
23–4) to share the interesting details of 'Lindholme, a reputed Hermit's
Cell, near Hatfield in Yorkshire; in whose grave was found a peck of
hemp-seed.' George Stovin (Tomlinson 1868: 75) wrote:*

The people of *Hatfield* and places adjacent have a tradition, that
on the middle of Hatfield waste there formerly liv'd an antient
Hermit who was called *William of Lindholme*; he was by the
common people take for a cunning man or conjurer, but in order
to be better informed, I, accompanyed with the Rev. Mr *Sam
Wesley* and others, went to view the place, and after passing
the morass, found the hermitage or cell situate in the middle
of 60 acres of firm sandy ground full of pebbles, on which was
growing barley, oats and pease. There was likewise a well 4 or
5 yards deep, full of clear spring water, which is very remark-
able, because the water of the morass is of the colour of coffee …
At the east end stood an altar made of hewn stone, and at the west
is the hermit's grave cover'd with a free stone that measures in
length 8 foot and a half, in breadth 3, and in thickness 8, which …
we rais'd up, and remov'd; and digging under found a tooth,
a scull, the thigh and shin bones of a human body, all of a very
large size; we likewise found in the grave a peck of hemp-seed,
and a beaten piece of copper … It is difficult to imagine how such
vast stones should be brought …

The same issue of the Gentleman's Magazine *features the following verse by Abraham de la Pryme (1671–1704), the antiquarian
and priest who lived and worked in the Axholme area for most
of his short life. He was briefly curate at Thorne, and was buried
at Hatfield.*

Within an humble lonesome cell
He free from care, and noise does dwell,
No pomp, no pride, no cursèd strife
Disturbs the quiet of his life,

A truss or two of straw's his bed,
His arms, the pillow for his head,
His hunger makes his bread go down
Altho' it be both stale and brown,
A purling brook that runs hard by
Affords him drink whene'er he's dry,
In short a Garden and a Spring
Does all life's necessaries bring.
What is't the foolish world call's poor?
He has enough; he needs no more;
No anxious thoughts corrode his breast,
No passions interrupt his rest,
No chilling fear, no hot desire,
Freezes or sets his blood on fire,
No tempest is engender'd there,
All does serene and calm appear,
And 'tis his comfort when alone
Seeing no ill, to think of none,
He spends each moment of his breath
In preparations for his death,
And patiently expects his doom
When fate shall order it to come.
He sees the wingéd lightning fly
Thro' the tempestuous angry sky,
And unconcern'd its thunder hears,
Who knows no guilt, can feel no fears.

William Henderson (1973 (1866): 118) mentions that 'ague' [i.e. marsh fever or malaria] was a common disease, particularly in fens and marshes, and 'has always been deemed peculiarly open to the influence of charms'. Marsh fever crops up frequently in the Lincolnshire folk tales collected nearby, by Mrs M.C. Balfour in the Folklore *journal; fear of something similar may underlie the story of this healing well. See Chapter 6, 'The Hangman Stone'.*

Tomlinson 1868.

LINDHOLME WILLIE

William's name resurfaces, centuries later, as a very modern ghost. Several varying versions of the story of 'Lindholme Willie' (or 'Billy') are told. Clive Kristen (1998) describes how, 'In 1947 a tall red-haired figure in an aircrew uniform was seen walking in a marsh area close to RAF Lindholme near Doncaster. Since this debut manifestation, "Lindholme Willie" has been sighted on a number of occasions.'

Kristen goes on to report an encounter with Lindholme Willie around Christmas 1967, by a couple – Peter and Jennifer Wharton – who saw the figure of an airman in a pub car park, and hailed him without getting a response. When they mentioned this curious circumstance to the landlord, he was clearly rather concerned – he poured a brandy, ran out, and offered it to the figure of the airman, which was still clearly visible. The airman seemed to accept the offer, but then faded away.

In Kristen's account, the landlord then tells the story of Lindholme Willie to the Whartons. The landlord was a child at the time and his parents were the licensees. He remembers the events as follows:

Willie was a Polish refugee, known only by his nickname. He was a regular in the pub, and a keen darts player. One night, a Lancaster bomber crashed in Hatfield Waste, with the loss of the whole crew.

The night after the crash, the landlady – the narrator's mother – had glimpsed Willie waiting outside the pub for another darts player to turn up, as was his habit. She sent her son out to him with a glass of brandy. But the boy brought the glass back; the street was empty, and Willie was gone.

About half an hour later, another group of airmen arrived to drink and play darts, and revealed that Willie was missing, presumed dead; he had been one of the crew of the crashed bomber.

5

LEGENDS OF
THE HALLS

THE HOMECOMING OF LEONARD RERESBY

When Leonard Reresby rode out from Thrybergh Hall to fight in the Crusades, he told his wife that he would return in seven years.

'If I am alive,' he told her, 'I will return. If I do not return, I will be dead, and you will be free to marry again.'

All the people heard him, and cheered him as he rode away.

He rode to the East, and made war with a good will against the enemies of his Church. In time he was taken prisoner and left in chains in a Turkish dungeon. In the confusion of the times there was no hope of ransom, but the Sultan did not care to slaughter Christian knights as if they were mere nobodies, and so he was left.

Seven long years Lady Reresby passed alone; alone in her house, alone in her bed, spending her days being both mother and father to her own children, lady and lord of her husband's lands. The war for the Church had been a strange and remote thing to her.

At first, in his prison, Leonard Reresby prayed for release; then for courage; finally, he abandoned hope and lived from moment to moment. The graces of his knightly breeding left him. He became a ragged, wild-eyed beggar, grateful enough to be left in peace to gnaw on a discarded crust. Every day he expected death. But his captors did not kill him.

Seven years passed, and Lady Reresby realised within herself that what was done was done. The estate needed a lord. The servants needed a master. The family needed a head and the children needed a father. The future lay open before her like the aisle of a church. There were good men aplenty in the district: sober, upright, dependable men whom any woman would be proud to call husband.

And still, every day, Leonard Reresby would make another mark on his dungeon wall. One day he reckoned up the marks by the sunlight through the window-bars, and saw that seven years had passed. And he remembered his promise: *If I do not return, I will be dead, and you will be free to marry again.*

'And I am alive,' he muttered. He closed his eyes. 'Dead indeed I might as well be. I have watched for this day in vain.'

And then, suddenly, with no further word than that, his stomach turned over, and his eyes opened.

Leonard Reresby was in Thrybergh, on the green slopes that led from the summit of East Hill in Thrybergh field, down towards the church where the bells were ringing. A light drizzle blew on his face, cooling the hot dust of the prison that still clung to him. He was alive; and he was home. And Thrybergh bells were ringing for a wedding.

At that sound, terror seized him afresh, and he took a tottering step towards the church; but he fell flat on his face with a heavy clank. Dazed, he picked himself up and squinted down, only to see Turkish shackles were still on his feet.

There was nothing for it. Squinting and muttering, he limped down the hill.

Meanwhile, within the church, Lady Reresby, in her widow's weeds, was approaching the altar where her bridegroom waited.

She was almost at the altar when behind her she heard the church door scrape open, and a hoarse cry. The people gasped and turned, and the bride turned with them, to see a ragged, emaciated figure, wild-eyed and loaded with chains, swaying in the doorway.

There was no wedding in Thrybergh that day. The Reresbys made their peace with the affronted bridegroom and his family, and – once Leonard was fully restored to health and happiness, and harmony with his neighbours – he hung his old chains up in the church, for any to see who wished to learn his story, and give thanks with him for the miracle. The chains hung in the church at Thrybergh for many years, and a stone cross was set in Thrybergh field, at the very place where Leonard's chained feet had first come to stand once again on the green fields of home.

St Leonard's Cross at Thrybergh

This story is a local version of a widespread theme of the homecoming hero. H. Leigh Bennett, in the Sheffield Miscellany, *gives the source as Sir John Reresby, a prominent monarchist in Commonwealth times. So the story may be a Reresby family legend and/or a popular tradition in Thrybergh. The Reresbys were the local landowners from the early fourteenth century until they gambled the estate away in the later seventeenth. In fact they do not seem to have fought in any Crusades. It may be inspired by the fittings at the church at Thrybergh, which was dedicated to St Leonard, and – although Reresby supposedly regarded Thrybergh's St Leonard as a separate figure – chains were the emblem of St Leonard of Noblac, patron of prisoners. Bennett records that there was a stained-glass window of St Leonard at the church. St Leonard's Cross was said to stand in the East Field at Thrybergh, allegedly marking the spot where Leonard came to land. Bennett also gives a ballad version of the story.*

Bett 1950: 19.

HAWORTH HALL

Haworth (or Howarth) Hall stood on Canklow Meadows near Rotherham, now an industrial estate and retail park. It was in existence by the early seventeenth century.

The last occupants of Haworth Hall were the Mountain family. Some family members believed their home to be haunted. Symptoms included heavy footsteps, rattling doors, and the audible rustle of clothing; the spirit was regarded by the Mountains as friendly and harmless. No disturbance of any kind was experienced or reported by several of the hall's previous occupants, including a former owner, Charles Tomlinson.

It was said, moreover, that a 'closely written vellum book' had been found at the hall, telling the story of a double murder there during the Elizabethan religious persecutions. The manuscript was supposedly discovered by Cecilia Kitson, a member of the tenant family, who had inadvertently triggered a disguised latch built into the hearth, and uncovered a forgotten priest-hole behind it, containing a skeleton stretched on a bed – and the manuscript. The remains were supposedly those of the manuscript's author, Wilfrid Haworth, a Catholic priest who had starved to death centuries before, while hiding from agents of the Protestant government. He had written the story in his final agony. The story he had to tell – which Cecilia Kitson is supposed to have translated and checked against other records as evidence – was grisly enough, for all its flowery style. We reproduce it here – ruthlessly trimmed and edited.

I, Wilfrid Haworth, priest of the holy Catholic Church, hereby record my last testament, in the hope that some day, my poor body may get Christian burial.

When the terrible Protestant persecution broke out against our Holy Church, our family held to our ancient Catholic faith, and our home was searched many times by the agents of the Crown. Priest as I was, it was only by using this secret hiding-place that I could escape arrest. Many times I hid behind the intricately designed trapdoor behind the fireplace, but there was one fatal flaw in its construction, and even that was thought an advantage: it could not be worked from the inside.

All might have been well, but for the mad jealousy of Sir Hubert Vayne of Tickhill Grange. He loved my sweet and beautiful sister, Elaine, with a mad passion that would not brook denial. Elaine detested him, and betrothed herself to our near neighbour, Sir George Kennard of Canklow House. When he heard the news, Sir Hubert set about his revenge, against Elaine and her whole family.

First, he caused my aged father to be arrested as a Catholic, and taken in chains to Pomfret Castle. My brothers, Oswald and Edmund, were both charged by Hubert Vayne, and both suffered for a crime of which they were innocent. He knew I was a priest, living in daily fear of arrest and execution, and set many a trap to catch me, but I mercifully escaped his vile plotting.

And then, one fateful day, I was tracked by a company of soldiers to the very hall itself. Elaine my sister and I were alone in the house, and with her help I was scarcely able to get into the hiding place behind the fireplace when Hubert Vayne strode into the room. Safe behind my prison walls I could hear what passed.

'How now,' said the villain, 'where is that brother of thine, the heretic priest?'

'Where thou canst not hurt him,' was Elaine's spirited reply.

Then I could hear Sir Hubert sound the walls, panel by panel. At last he grew tired, and ceased his search. Then, for some dreadful reason, the villain lost all restraint of himself. 'I swear to thee, Elaine, Sir George shall never wed thee!'

From my cunning hole in the mantel I could see murder in the villain's face, yes, and foul murder it was. He sprang at her, and despite my loud cry of warning, the foul deed was done. Poor Elaine lay there, weltering in her virgin blood at the murderer's feet. Priest as I am, all my passion of manhood came back to me, and I called out 'Murderer!'

At last he found voice and courage to say, 'So, my fine rebel priest, I have slain the only one of thy family who knows the mystery of thy hiding place, so much the better for me, and so much the worse for thee. Rot in thy priest hole. None shall come nigh to whom thou mayst tell the secret of its opening.'

With that he took up the body of my sister and went forth, I know not whither, or to what hellish work.

The end is nigh; God is good. I feel no pain; the hunger is gone; to God I commend my spirit, I pray for him who did the wrong. Lord Jesus, receive my soul.

This tale of Gothic horror might seem to be a fake legend, but at its centre there seems to be a grain, not of truth exactly, but of genuine folk legend. In the 1960s, a shale quarrying operation at Treeton uncovered 'a hole or tunnel, situated in the side of the hill', which the local 'old codgers' explained as 'a priest's escape passage' that led 'directly underground, right under the meadows to Howarth Hall'. One of them claimed to have walked the tunnel in his youth, and used up three or four candles without reaching the end of it. This suggests that the story of Cecilia Kitson's manuscript may be built on real local tradition, or something like it.

Canklow Meadows is now a retail and business park. The hall was
demolished in the mid-1960s to make way for an electricity substation,
which now stands hard by the A630 Rotherway where it crosses the
Rother on the approach to Junction 33 on the M1.

Sheffield Star 27-5-1959, 28-9-1965 (RALS); *Rotherham Advertiser*
31-12-1971, 7-1-1972, 4-2-1972, 11-2-1972, 21-4-1972 (RALS).

THE GREEN LADY OF FIRBECK HALL

John West was head of the West family and master of Firbeck Hall:
a sour-tempered, grasping man, and a confirmed bachelor. If he
died without issue – as he was expected to – one of his sisters,
Catherine or Elizabeth, would inherit. If that sister married, her
husband would be master of the hall.

West was watching his sisters closely and quietly.

All this took place more than three hundred years ago, and,
when the Civil War broke out between king and Parliament, John
West decided that his family would be taking the king's side.

Firbeck Hall

'Property,' he said. 'If they start dragging the king off his throne, next thing, they'll be putting the gentry out of their houses. I will not allow it. We will serve our king, and defend our property.'

West trusted few of his servants, but with those few he was very close. Among his favourites was the head gardener. One day, as the war raged from south to north, the head gardener at Firbeck Hall came to John West in secret, and whispered that his sister Catherine had been meeting a young man in the grounds of the hall. They were meeting in secret, the man said, on a yew-lined path on the estate, known as the Dark Walk.

As soon as he heard these words, John West considered that the Dark Walk was well hidden from the windows of the hall, with a waterfall emptying into a lake behind, beneath an ornamental bridge, loudly enough to mask any noise. It was a perfect place for a secret meeting.

The next evening, when he noticed that his sister was preparing to leave the house, everything in his mind fell into place. He remembered Catherine's comings and goings over the last few weeks, and saw exactly when, and where, and how she might have been going out to meet her secret lover on the Dark Walk – going out to meet the heir of the hall, as one day he might well be, if matters proceeded to marriage.

And so John West waited until she was out of the house, and then he cloaked himself and crept out of the house after his sister, and followed her at a distance to the Dark Walk, over the bridge and down past the mill by the pond under the yew trees.

He waited, well hidden in the shadows, and watched.

Soon, West heard, and half-saw, a man come from the direction of St Martin's church. His tread was light and his manner was that of a young man. John West watched as the newcomer took Catherine in his arms, and kissed her, and greeted her with words of love.

As soon as West heard and recognised the man's voice, he knew that the man was Ralph Knight of Langold. His sister had done worse than go behind his back: she had betrayed the whole family, and the king's cause. For Knight was a Commonwealth man and a colonel in Cromwell's New Model Army.

John West stalked back to his hall, incandescent with rage. It was unthinkable to him that Knight could possibly love his sister. It was a ploy: a ploy to get his rebel hands on Firbeck Hall.

John West ordered his most trusted servants to watch for the next time Catherine seemed to be preparing to make her secret journey. When they alerted him, he had them detain her at the hall on some pretext.

Then, still furious, he made his way to the Dark Walk.

As he approached, he saw that Ralph Knight was awaiting his lover beneath the yew trees of the Dark Walk. When he saw a robed figure approaching, he opened his arms, ready to embrace Catherine.

But Ralph looked up to see the face of John West, and it was the last thing he saw.

John West, now a murderer, left his enemy dead on the dirty ground of the Dark Walk, in a pool of his own cooling blood. He managed to stumble back to the hall, his rage ebbing and a dull horror descending on him; but, as he did, he saw Catherine, hastening from the hall towards the Dark Walk. She was alone; clearly, she had shaken off the servants. Her brow was furrowed and she was more agitated than she evidently wanted to seem.

They passed each other on the narrow path without a word. There was nothing John West could do or say. With as much of a false smile as he could muster, he nodded to his sister as she passed.

Then, from an upstairs window at the hall, he watched her hastening eagerly through the grounds towards the Dark Walk, and disappearing under the yew trees.

He never saw his sister alive again.

When Catherine West's body was found and drawn from the lake, the weed clung to her from the stagnant waters, and it was a hard job for the servants to bring her to the bank. Ralph Knight still lay in his blood, close at hand; Catherine West had left her lover's side for the last time, to make her marriage bed alone in the cold waters of the lake.

History records that John West died without issue in 1657, and Firbeck Hall passed to Francis Fane, husband of Elizabeth West. A memorial to Ralph Knight can still be found in St Martin's churchyard, and Catherine West – so they say – can still be seen from time to time, on the Dark Walk where the yew trees stood, trapped behind a ghostly green veil, still awaiting her lover's return.

The Firbeck estate is medieval, but the present Firbeck Hall was built in 1594 by William West, a rich and successful lawyer, and held by his family for several generations. By the early seventeenth century, the hall and estate were the property of William's grandson, John West. This is our version of a story that is common knowledge in Firbeck, where one of us (DB) heard it. The Green Lady's tomb is said to lie among a cluster of graves in St Martin's churchyard, although these graves lack inscriptions.

Rotherham Advertiser 1-8-2003 (RALS); *Worksop Guardian* 5-11-1993 (RALS).

The White Deer of Parkwood Springs

Parkwood Springs in Sheffield, overlooking the upper Don Valley, was an ancient deer park. Long ago, a white deer was born to the herd. The lord of the manor took this as an ill omen, and wanted the white deer killed. In this, he was following received wisdom: white deer are known as 'Judas deer', because, even in darkness, their colour betrays the herd to hunters, predators and poachers, and, for these and other less practical reasons, they are seen as bringers of bad luck. But the lady of the manor wanted the white deer spared. She begged her husband to spare the deer's life. It was to no avail, however; the lord was obeyed, and the white deer was hunted down and slaughtered.

Who knows what drove the lady to attach such importance to the life of a single beast? If it was a sense of foreboding, it proved to be well founded. Shortly after the white deer was hunted down, the lady gave birth to a son, but the child was lost. To this day, around Pitsmoor and Shirecliffe, you will hear it said that bad luck will follow for anyone who sees a white deer roaming on Parkwood Springs.

This story was told to Shonaleigh, a professional storyteller who for many years worked with local communities on the Beacons festival, an annual storytelling event based around Parkwood Springs. It was told by a resident of Jasmine Court Nursing Home, as part of work for the Beacons festival around 2010. Shonaleigh suggests that the story as she tells it may be missing some detail. Certainly Parkwood Springs was an old deer park, and there are several stories of white deer as beasts of ill omen and/or magical power at Levens Hall in Cumbria, Eagle Crag in West Yorkshire, and elsewhere.

The Madness of Thomas Wortley

A local legend accuses … Thomas [Wortley] of having destroyed a village to clear his hunting-ground between Wharncliffe and Penistone, in punishment for which deed he eventually went mad, and 'belled' like a stag.

Armitage 1897: 8n.

6

LEGENDS OF THE ROADS

THE HANGMAN STONE

Hangman Stone Road runs by Melton Wood, between the Barnsley and Doncaster roads, skirting the foot of Ludwell Hill. There is a story told of the way that it obtained its curious name.

A thief once took a sheep, and in order to get it away as quickly and quietly as possible, he tied its forelegs and hind legs all together, slung it around his neck, and set off on foot.

In this way he was passing down Hangman Stone Road, and came to the Hangman Stone itself. Gaunt and dark and still it stood in the moonlight. What the stone was, and why it stood where it stood, the thief never once stopped to think. All he saw was a place where he could rest, without loosing his grip on his prize.

He backed up to the stone, and laid the bound sheep on its side on its uppermost face. The weight of the beast left his straining back. Here, he thought, he could gain some respite.

But the body of the sheep slid off the far side of the stone. And the thief was caught, for the beast's bound feet were still slung round his neck, and he was caught on one side of the stone while the sheep slid down the other, and the knots at its hooves tightened round the man's throat. He knew what was happening, but it would have taken several men to lift the sheep. There was nothing he could do. He was found strangled in the morning, sitting at the foot of the Hangman Stone.

This story was published in September 1899 in Notes and Queries, *the famous magazine that functioned in the nineteenth century as a kind of compendium and discussion group for folklore and other matters of general interest. It was said to have occurred in the reign of Charles II.*

Hangman Stone Road still exists by that name, but the actual stone, and its location, are lost. The story is a migratory legend – that is, a story that is told of several different places. Correspondents to Notes and Queries *were quick to point out that South Yorkshire itself also had other variants of the same story, with reference to a Hangman's Stone in Tankersley, south of Barnsley. They seem to have meant either the Birdwell Obelisk, or Queen Anne's Obelisk in Rainborough Park. There is also a Hangmanstone Depot in Birdwell.*

In the course of this correspondence, F.H. Newman lets slip the following interesting information:

> Hangman's Hill, near Thorne, got its name from being the place of the execution of some rioters, who had made a violent assault on the labourers employed in draining Hatfield Chase, in the reign of Charles I.

For more on Hatfield Chase, see the story of St William of Lindholme.

SWIFT NICK NEVISON

Throughout the 1600s, England fought many wars of conquest in other peoples' homelands. Once the wars were over, back came the soldiers, hardened in spirit and wounded in body and mind.

Small wonder, then, if highwaymen in England in those days were as common as crows. Few, if any, were gallant, or generous, or squeamish about bloodshed, or gentlemanly. Few, if any, were loyal to friends, or courteous to women, or concerned with fair play or mercy.

But one of them was. And he was a South Yorkshireman, and he went by a nickname that a king gave him. People called him *Swift Nick*.

Some say Swift Nick's true name was John Nevison; others say he was William. Some say he was the son of a wool merchant, others of a steward at Wortley Hall. But he was a high-spirited youth, and he left school under a cloud, and then he made his way to London, where he worked for a time as a brewer's clerk. One day, the brewer sent him with instructions to collect on a debt. Young John collected the money just as he had been told to, then he ran off with it to the Netherlands, and lived riotously until it ran out. He enlisted as a soldier, serving with distinction in Flanders, and returned to England, and lived quietly.

But then his father died, and he was left quite alone, facing a lifetime of hopeless poverty. And so he took to the road.

SWIFT NICK'S NAME

One morning before dawn, in 1676, Nevison robbed a sailor at Gad's Hill, near Rochester. The sailor shook his fist, and shouted that he knew Nevison when he saw him. That would be enough to hang him, and any other highwayman would have killed the man to silence him. But Nevison had long ago decided that he had shed enough blood for one lifetime already. It would take a miracle of skulduggery to save the foolhardy sailor, and so Nevison decided that he would work the miracle.

He left the man cursing and spluttering in the road, and set off northwards, riding at a good pace towards the Thames. He took the ferry at dawn and turned his horse's head for Chelmsford. As morning passed, he flew like a shadow in the daylight across the flat country towards Cambridge, and as the noonday sun looked down on Huntingdon, he found the Great North Road at last. There he turned northwards.

Nevison rode through the gates of York as the sun set, having ridden steadily, and rested regularly, and made two hundred and thirty miles in one single day. It was an astonishing feat of horsemanship.

'And the pity of it is,' Nevison told himself ruefully, 'I shall never be able to tell anyone about it. Perhaps one day word will get out, but by that time I will be hanged, or dead of old age. Probably some other man will claim the credit.'

He changed his clothes and stabled his horse at the York Inn, and as the bells of York Minster rang eight o'clock, Nevison stepped on to the bowling green at York, in full view of many respectable public men and witnesses, and greeted the Lord Mayor of York so heartily that the Mayor was forced to pretend that he knew who Nevison was. In full view of the crowds they chatted like old friends for a while, and then Nevison idly picked up a bowling ball and casually mentioned the possibility of a game of bowls.

'No gentleman would refuse a game,' the Mayor assured him.

'Indeed not. And what would a game be, Lord Mayor,' Nevison inquired, 'without a wager?'

The coins jingled enticingly in the moneybag at Nevison's waist, and the Mayor found himself placing a larger sum than he had intended on the outcome of the game. This worried him, for he was not really a betting man; nor, truth to be told, was he much of a bowler, but it quickly became clear that his strange but friendly opponent was no mean sportsman at all. The Mayor was secretly relieved beyond measure when he won the game, seemingly more by luck than judgment, and pocketed the handsome stakes. He took pity on the man and treated him to wine, and the Mayor and his new friend Mr Nevison parted the best of friends.

The next day but one, after a furious pursuit and hurried exchange of post-notes and whispers up and down the Great North Road, a troop of redcoats arrived from Essex, tumbled Nevison out of his bed at the York Inn, and put him on trial for his life. The sailor identified Nevison by sight on the spot, and swore to it, and Nevison looked very likely to hang.

The prospect seemed to amuse him, in a quiet way, and he called no witnesses for the defence except one: the Lord Mayor of York.

There was a stir in the courtroom, but the Mayor took the stand, and Nevison asked him if he knew the name of the man who was addressing him.

'I should hope I did,' the Mayor said. 'You're Mr Nevison, from the York Inn.'

'And when did we last meet?'

'On the bowling green, at eight o'clock, Thursday last,' the Lord Mayor said.

'And what were we doing there?'

'Playing bowls,' the Mayor said, basking privately in the memory of his game. 'I remember it quite distinctly, because –'

But Nevison had already turned away.

'And can it be,' he demanded, 'gentlemen of the jury, that a man who was playing bowls on the green at York at eight o'clock on Thursday night robbed a traveller in Kent on Thursday morning?'

There was laughter in court, and Nevison left the court a free man.

And it turned out as he had predicted: word got out. How, we will never know. But with the law of double jeopardy, Nevison had little to fear from rumour, and did little to quash it. And the rumour, in time, reached the ears of the king, Charles Stuart. And Charles was greatly amused, and said that he would like to meet this Swift Nick.

Whether he ever did or not, we cannot say, but in any case the nickname stuck.

SWIFT NICK AND THE HIGHWAYMEN

Swift Nick Nevison was scouring the roads one day when he met two farmers coming the other way, who warned him not to go ahead. They had been robbed by three highwaymen about half a mile back. Nevison asked them how much they had lost, and they told him forty pounds.

'That won't do, honest men such as yourselves. Turn back with me, and show me the way they took, and I'll deal with them,' Nick told them.

Greatly heartened, the farmers turned back, and followed Swift Nick as he forged ahead. Before too long they overtook a lone rider.

'That's one of the villains,' the farmer said. 'I'd know him anywhere.'

'They'll have split up, then,' Swift Nick said.

Ordering the farmers to stay back at a distance, he rode up.

'You, sir,' he said, 'have borrowed forty pounds from two friends of mine, I think; and I have come, as a favour to them, to secure repayment of the loan.'

'Damn you, sir,' the highwayman exclaimed frankly, 'are you not mad, to ask such a thing?'

'Mad enough. Be sure of that,' Nick rejoined calmly, jamming the muzzle of a loaded pistol between his waistcoat buttons.

The man was soon begging for his life, and Nick was only too happy to grant it.

'Calm yourself, sir. Your life's not worth threepence to me,' Swift Nick explained. 'I would never stoop to rob a man of so little. Just the forty pounds, sir, if you please.'

The main explained that he had divided the spoils with his two accomplices, and they had ridden on ahead, leaving him with only twenty pounds.

'No trouble; I'll have the twenty,' Nick said. 'And your pistols, and your horse and coat.'

He put the man's coat on, and tied him to his horse in his shirt, and led him by the bridle back to the two farmers. Then, leaving him prisoner with the delighted farmers, he mounted the highwayman's horse, and rode on after the other two rogues.

When the other two rogues saw him coming, on their friend's horse, in their friend's coat, they naturally enough took him for the man himself. By the time they realised their mistake, it was too late; Nick was upon them, with two loaded pistols ready to hand.

'Gentlemen,' said Nick, 'I have come as a favour from your friend, whose coat and horse I have been forced to borrow, as an elementary precaution. He is currently held prisoner by some trustworthy friends of mine. Please believe me when I say that I have but to give the word, and he will hang without trial. And then you and I will immediately settle the matter with sword and pistol. If, however, you give me the twenty pounds freely, you have my word that I'll have him released, and we three can part as friends.'

The thieves were not so easily talked around, and they drew pistols and fired; but the shot went wide, giving Nick time to return fire. Nick was the better shot, and once the foremost thief had Swift Nick's bullet in his arm, he quickly begged terms.

Swift Nick frowned.

'It will cost you rather more than twenty pounds now, I am afraid,' he said.

He took all they had – a hundred and fifty pounds in all. Then, being a man of his word, he released all three highwaymen without further nuisance. As they galloped off down the road, happy enough to have got away from Swift Nick Nevison with their lives, Nick himself quietly handed the forty pounds over to the farmers.

'And if you wish to be good friends to me, as I have been to you,' he told the farmers, 'then I ask no more than a measure of discretion on your part, should the magistrates ever seek news of Swift Nick Nevison.'

The farmers took the hint, and winked and bowed, and with many protestations of gratitude they parted company. And Nick rode on alone, wondering idly if either the farmers or the highwaymen had been following matters closely enough to notice how much richer a man he himself was from the day's dealings.

SWIFT NICK'S DEATH

Swift Nick met with an early death; so early, in fact, that it preceded the actual end of his life by some years.

The law caught up with him, and he was taken in irons to Leicester Gaol. Prisons were death traps in Swift Nick's days, and it was not long before the rumour went out that Swift Nick Nevison had been taken with a pestilence. Swift Nick was taken to a cell with a little more air, but neither gaoler nor prisoners would go nearer to him than the door of his cell.

His many friends and visitors meanwhile waited on him, and went in and out of his cell at will, as if he had no fever at all. But their heroic efforts seemed unavailing. Word soon went out that Swift Nick had cheated the hangman and died. Weeping inconsolably, Swift Nick's friends called for the jury to determine the cause of death, as the law required. The terrified jurors stood at the door of the cell, saw the highwayman's motionless body covered in blue spots, and pronounced Swift Nick dead of the plague. No gaoler would touch the corpse, and Swift Nick's friends had to sew him up in a makeshift shroud and carry him out of the prison gate, where, once they were round the corner and out of sight, Nick leapt up out of his shroud and headed off to the nearest tavern, complaining that death of the plague had given him a terrible thirst.

For, of course, Swift Nick was in perfect health. His huddle of friends had painted blue plague-spots all over him, and fed him enough doctored gin to render him pleasantly comatose. But there's no rumour like a rumour driven by fear; few on the roads could be brought to believe that Swift Nick was anything but dead of the plague, even weeks later, after many a coach had been robbed by the ghost of Swift Nick Nevison.

SWIFT NICK'S PRAISE

Swift Nick Nevison was hanged at York on 4 May 1685. He was buried in an unmarked grave in St Mary's church, York. He was forty-five years old. It was a good age for a highwayman and he had had a good run.

He ran a gang of thieves out of the Talbot Inn at Newark, and lived by robbery along the Great North Road. From York to Huntingdon, no coach was safe from him. He was arrested several times, and escaped several times. But in the end, he seems to have broken his own rule, and shed blood. Men accustomed to violence will often grow too impatient of any restraint – even the best of them, after a time – they will weary, and be foolishly careless of their own lives and the lives of others. Then they are best avoided, for their company is dangerous, even to their friends, and their lives are likely to be squandered, and short.

However it happened, Swift Nick killed a man, a constable named Fletcher who was trying to arrest him, and then there was a price on his head. He was taken while drinking at the Magpie Inn in Sandal, near Wakefield, after the landlady had tipped off the bounty hunters for a share of the price.

Once he was dead, broadside and ballad went to work in Swift Nick's praise, as they had done for centuries, for many a thief in South Yorkshire and beyond; and that praise lasted so long that we can still hear one of the voices that was raised to proclaim it. In 1908, the folk song collector Percy Grainger recorded the virtuoso traditional singer Joseph Taylor, on the brand new technology of wax cylinders. The cylinders have survived, and so we can still hear the voice of Joseph Taylor, still strong and clear in his eighties, towards the end of a long life as a farm bailiff, singing the old song of 'Bold Nevison':

> Did you ever hear tell of that hero,
> Bold Nevison that was his name?
> He rode about like a bold hero,
> and with that he gained great fame.

> He maintained himself like a gentleman;
> besides he was good to the poor.
> He rode about like a bold hero,
> and he gain'd himself favour therefore.

> Oh the twenty-first day of last month
> proved an unfortunate day;
> Captain Milton was riding to London,
> and by mischance he rode out of his way.

> He call'd at a house by the road-side,
> it was the sign of the *Magpie*,
> where Nevison he sat a drinking,
> and the captain soon did he espy.

> Then a constable very soon was sent for,
> and a constable very soon came;
> with three or four more in attendance,
> with pistols charged in the king's name.

They demanded the name of this hero;
'My name it is Johnson,' said he.
When the captain laid hold of his shoulder.
Saying, 'Nevison, thou goeth with me.'

Oh! Then in this very same speech
they hastened him fast away
to a place call'd Swinnington bridge,
A place where he used to stay.

They call'd for a quart of good liquor.
It was the sign of the *Black Horse*
where there was all sorts of attendance,
But for Nevison it was the worst.

He call'd for a pen, ink, and paper,
And these were the words that he said:
'I will write for some boots, shoes, and stockings,
For of them I have very great need.'

'Tis now before my lord judge.
Oh! 'Guilty or not do you plead?'
He smiled into the judge and jury
and these were the words that he said:

'I've now robb'd a gentleman of two pence;
I've neither done murder nor kill'd;
but guilty I've been all my life time,
So, gentlemen, do as you will.

'It's when that I rode on the highway
I've always had money in great store;
and whatever I took from the rich
I freely gave it to the poor.

> 'But my peace I have made with my Maker,
> and with you I'm quite ready to go;
> so here's adieu! to this world and its vanities,
> for I'm ready to suffer the law.'

We first heard about Swift Nick Nevison from the novelist Chris Nickson. Our main source of stories about this is the Newgate Calendar,[27] *the hugely popular and influential collection of real-life tales of crime and punishment in the decades around 1800. Ostensibly, the* Calendar *was supposed to teach children the horrible consequences of a life of crime, but children loved it for the lurid thrills, and it made household names of figures like Captain Kidd, Dick Turpin, the Tolpuddle Martyrs, and many others.*

Swift Nick's most famous adventure, the high-speed ride to York, is not in the Calendar, *so we have taken it from an excellent website, Stand and Deliver![28] Credit for this incredible feat of horsemanship was first given to Dick Turpin in a 1739 biography of Turpin, and made popular by William Harrison Ainsworth in his 1834 novel* Rookwood. *But Turpin did not do it. Although he is almost forgotten today, Ainsworth was a hugely popular novelist in his own lifetime, and many legends that are now commonly accepted have their origins in his imagination.*

Joseph Taylor's folk song 'Bold Nevison' is featured on the Leader LP Unto Brigg Fair *(Taylor 1972). It has been covered by several modern folk singers. A full version of the lyric is given in Ingledew's* Yorkshire Ballads *(1860: 125–28), which is the basis of our text.*

> Cf. 'Mainly Norfolk: English Folk and other Good Music',
> www.informatik.uni-hamburg.de/~zierke/joseph.taylor/
> songs/boldnevison.html, accessed 10-1-2015.

---

27 *Newgate Calendar*, www.exclassics.com/newgate/ngintro.htm, accessed 10-1-2015.

28 'Stand and Deliver!' www.stand-and-deliver.org.uk, accessed 10-1-2015.

7

SHEFFIELD
HOUSEHOLD TALES

Sidney Oldall Addy (1848–1933) worked as a solicitor, but his passion was the folklore, history, dialect and archaeology of his home city and its environs. Born into an affluent capitalist family in Norton, and educated at Oxford, he lived and worked in Sheffield for most of his long life, producing many acclaimed and ground-breaking books and articles. His major work on traditional narrative is the Household Tales and Traditional Remains *of 1895, the basis of which is a collection of fifty-two tales collected from storytellers in Lincolnshire, Derbyshire, Nottinghamshire, and Yorkshire, in the years around 1890. Here we include the tales which Addy collected from South Yorkshire, or which he made a point of associating with the area.*

Many of these tales are English variants of international folk tale types, widely told throughout Europe and North America, and Addy himself regarded his research as no more than a scratch on the surface of a substantial local tradition. In 1973 the Sheffield folklorist and linguist John Widdowson stated that the tradition was dead and that Addy's stories had mostly 'passed out of oral tradition'.

Addy's folktales are mysterious in several other ways besides. Firstly, he recorded virtually nothing about the storytellers he consulted; he was in the habit of describing tales as coming from places (such as Sheffield) rather than people. Nor did he record much about how he went about his research; he simply noted that he obtained all of his stories from 'oral tradition, and not from printed sources', and he either wrote the tales down himself 'from dictation' or received them as written copies. 'As far as I could manage it,' he added, 'the tales are given in the very words of the narrators,' although he admitted to translating some dialect to standard English.

Addy touched on the real mystery of the stories he collected when he described them as 'beautiful or highly humorous even in their decay,' illustrating 'the poverty of present tradition'. Folklorist Katharine Briggs regarded 'The Broken Pitcher' as a version of the Cinderella story (1991 (1970) Part A, Vol. 1: 172) – which illustrates the point, because it makes a very worn-down, fragmentary Cinderella. Addy could not guess how the stories came to take these odd but arresting forms. He could not even make up his mind whether he was dealing with complete stories, or partial fragments of tales that had once been more complete and better formed.

Nor can we. Perhaps the tradition he recorded really was in general decline. It may be that there was a point to the stories which Addy missed, and which we therefore struggle to catch ourselves.

THE FARMER AND HIS MAN

One day a farmer was walking round his farm, when he heard his man singing in a barn. So he stopped to listen and heard these words:

> Bread and cheese, work as you please,
> Bread and cheese, work as you please.

The farmer then went and told his wife what he had heard.

The farmer's wife asked, 'How did he seem to be working?'

'Oh,' he said, 'I peeped through a loophole in the barn, and he didn't see me; but I saw him, and he was working as slowly as he could.'

'That'll never do,' she said, 'I'll try him with something better than that.'

So the next day she made a nice plum pudding and an apple pie for the man. Then she told her husband to go and see if he worked any better.

> Plum pudden and apple pie,
> Do your work accordingly.
> Plum pudden and apple pie,
> Do your work accordingly.

So the farmer went back to his wife and told her what he had heard.

'How was he working?' she asked.

'Much better, but not so fast as he might do,' he replied.

'Oh, well,' she said. 'I'll try him with better food than that.'

So the next day she gave him roast beef and plum pudding, and told her husband to go and see if he worked any better.

This time the farmer heard him singing:

> Roast beef and plum pudden,
> Do your work like a good un.
> Roast beef and plum pudden,
> Do your work like a good un.

Then the farmer told his wife what he had heard, and said the man was working as hard as a horse, and with all his might.

So after this the farmer's wife always fed the man on the best food that she could get, and he worked hard ever after.

This tale was told to Addy's future wife, Mary Golden Parkin, by a nurse in Sheffield, around 1872. Addy published it in 'Four Yorkshire Tales', Folklore VIII (1897). It is reprinted in Katharine M. Briggs' A Dictionary of British Folk-Tales. We have reproduced it word for word.

Briggs 1991 (1970), Part A, Vol. 2: 81.

THE OLD MAN AT THE WHITE HOUSE

There was once a man who lived in a white house in a certain village, and he knew everything about everybody who lived in the place.

In the same village there lived a woman who had a daughter called Sally, and one day she gave Sally a pair of yellow gloves and threatened to kill her if she lost them.

Now Sally was very proud of her gloves, but she was careless enough to lose one of them. After she had lost it she went to a row of houses in the village and enquired at every door if they had seen her glove. But everybody said 'no', and she was told to go and ask the man who lived in the white house.

So Sally went to the white house and asked the old man if he had seen her glove. The old man said: 'I have thy glove, and I will give it thee if thou wilt promise to me to tell nobody where thou hast found it. And remember, if thou tells anybody I shall fetch thee out of bed when the clock strikes twelve at night.'

So he gave the glove back to Sally.

But Sally's mother got to know about her losing the glove, and asked her daughter, 'Where did you find it?'

Sally said, 'I daren't tell, for if I do the old man will fetch me out of bed at twelve o'clock at night.'

Her mother said, 'I will bar all the doors and fasten all the windows and then he can't get in and fetch thee,' and she made Sally tell her where she had found her glove.

So Sally's mother barred all the doors and fastened all the windows, and Sally went to bed at ten o'clock that night and began to cry. At eleven she began to cry louder, and at twelve o'clock she heard a voice saying in a whisper, but gradually getting louder and louder:

> Sally, I'm up one step.
> Sally, I'm up two steps.
> Sally, I'm up three steps.
> Sally, I'm up four steps.

Sally, I'm up five steps.

Sally, I'm up six steps.

Sally, I'm up seven steps.

Sally, I'm up eight steps.

Sally, I'm up nine steps.

Sally, I'm up ten steps.

Sally, I'm up eleven steps.

Sally, I'm up twelve steps!

Sally, I'm at thy bedroom door!!

SALLY, I HAVE HOLD OF THEE!!!

The teller of this tale was Richard Hirst of Sheffield, aged 18. Addy published it in 'Four Yorkshire Tales', Folklore VIII (1897). We have reproduced it word for word. The point of the story is obviously to make the listener jump – a popular genre of storytelling with older children and teenagers.

Briggs 1991 (1970), Part A, Vol. 2: 550–51.

THE KING IN THE FOREST

A long time ago, a girl lived with her father and mother in a town in a fork between two rivers.

Many times in her childhood, her father had forbidden her to venture into the deep wooded dales that split the hills beyond. The whole town shared his fear. Other children in the schoolyard and street would whisper among themselves that anyone who went up the dale would fall into the clutches of someone they simply called *the king*. They spoke so solemnly that the girl did not even ask who the king was, or what he wanted. Even when she asked her mother what lay behind the stories, her mother would only say one word: 'Moonshine.'

Years passed. One cool day, in late spring, for some reason or none, the girl quarrelled with her mother and found herself crossing the river, by narrow stepping stones behind the house-backs, and found the narrow path that wove up the dale between the curved walls of sunlit trees, into a whispering green silence.

The path was easy to keep to, and time passed quickly. The light was deadening, and the air was cooling before she realised that she had lost her way. She turned to retrace her steps, but her landmarks failed her, and before long, night was beginning to fall in earnest. She was soon stumbling and falling, scraping her knees on the rough path. By the time night fell completely, the girl was beyond terror, lonely and desperate for a way home.

Then the moon came out, and above and ahead in the half-darkness, she saw the roof of a tower, shadowed against a nest of oaks.

He heart leaped and her head swam. She pushed towards it, and found herself at a narrow gate in a wall, leading to a lawn. She passed through the gate and crossed to the foot of the tower at the end of the lawn. A grey light still burned in the upper windows.

Up the approach she ran, shivering in the bitter cold, and at last she drew the bell-pull in the porch.

A hatch opened in the door and a gnarled face with glittering eyes appeared. She looked up and gave the name of the town. The creased lips moved, and a voice intoned, 'Too soon'.

The hatch slid shut. There was silence.

She waited anxiously, and after a while, there was the sound of a bolt being drawn. The door was hauled back and the gnarled creature stepped back, latch in hand, to reveal a tall, dark figure with a pale face.

'Are you the king?' she asked, tentatively.

'I am.'

The figure turned, and moved back towards the hallway, and she sensed that the dark figure had something to tell her.

'Come.'

The figure led her along the hallway, and through a door under a ceiling so high that she could barely glimpse the rafters. The room she was shown to was large and gloomy, with a fireplace gaped in the moonlight. There was nothing else in the room besides a four-poster bed with hangings the colour of old dried blood. The figure pointed to the bed, and spoke again.

'Sleep.'

Then the latch dropped, and she was alone in the room. She kicked her shoes off and wrapped herself up in the coverlets, still in her clothes.

In the morning the air in the room was sharp. Pale spring sunlight streamed through the windows. She pulled her shoes on, and went off in search of some life. The whole house seemed derelict and bleak; every room seemed deserted, so she gave up, and made for the front door.

As she crossed the hall towards it, however, there was a movement in a side-doorway. A handsome, very solid-looking young man had suddenly appeared there, and was standing looking at her. He stood rather crookedly, but his unruly hair was flaming gold.

'Marry me,' he said at once, and grinned.

She turned to the door only to see a shape in the shadows: it was the dark figure, the king, and he was watching her.

The young man had already launched himself across the hallway with a grin, hands outstretched. He threw his arms round her and hauled her off her feet.

'You came too soon,' the dark figure said as she struggled to free herself. 'Now you must stay.'

She was dragged back through the narrow door from which the crooked man had come, and thrown down on the cellar floor.

As she lay on the cold earth, her eyes became accustomed to the shadows, and she began to discern a stained skylight above. A smear of light was streaming through the thick air towards the earthen floor. Then, in the dim light from the window, she discerned the form of a woman in blue, looking coolly down at her; and the woman spoke.

'Now you have seen,' the woman said. 'It is only moonshine. Come.' She seemed to hold a hand out.

The girl's fingers closed on the woman's hand with its golden ring, and she followed her back up the narrow stair. The cellar-door was already ajar. They passed through the empty hallway together, out of the tower, and across the lawn. When they were out again beyond the narrow gate in the wall, the girl turned to thank the woman. But the woman's face was already fading in the sunlight.

'Hang the ring from a thread, and remember. And go home.'

That was the last thing she said. The girl was alone, with nothing to hold on to but the gold ring. It seemed to tug at her hand and she followed where it pulled, towards the footpath and home.

Somewhere far behind her, dogs were beginning to bark busily. She hurried onwards. Before long she began to recognise the landmarks she had left, and she knew that she was on her way home. Still, far behind her, the hounds barked. The run back was surprisingly short, and soon she saw the spires and roofs of the town peering between the trunks of the last trees, just over the brow of the shimmering banks of bluebells. Falling to her knees, the ring and thread slipped out of her fingers as the distant barking faded to silence.

Day was dawning in the town, and over the river the cries of workers were beginning to fill the streets. She lingered, unwilling to be seen crossing back over the river, and realised that she had dropped the ring. She patted the turf down in search of it. But it was nowhere to be found among the flowers.

In the end, she had to give up searching, and made for the stepping stones.

The streets of the town seemed smaller, and she arrived home just as her mother was lighting the fire and making tea, amid the silence of the sleeping house.

Her mother glanced up at her from the fireplace, and caught the look in her eye.

'What's been the matter with you?' she demanded.

'Nothing,' the girl replied, and then added: 'Only moonshine.'

Her mother looked twice at her.

'Well,' she said, 'you're back at least.'

She said no more.

Addy 1895: 30–4

THE WOODSMAN AND THE HATCHET

A lord once told a woodsman to clear the trees by the deepest pool of the River Rivelin. The day before, as it happened, the woodsman had lost his axe in the very pool where his lord was sending him. He borrowed an axe from his cousin Edward and headed along the river to the place where he had been sent.

There he singled out a tree, and went to work with all his strength. At the third blow, a sharp pain shot down his arms, and he felt the handle of the axe grow lighter in his hands. Then he heard the inevitable splash, and when he looked, the head of the axe was nowhere to be seen. The water rippled and a dark cloud of dirt was rising from the riverbed. His heart sank.

There was no chance he was getting the axe-head back. Not today anyway, and certainly not in time to meet his lord's demands. He felt his back sliding down the very same tree.

Then he noticed an uncanny glow rising from the deepest regions of the river. An eerie cloud of shining turquoise emerged from the water, and skittered to and fro across its surface. The cloud of light settled directly before him and took on human form. The woodman was staring at what he could only have called a fairy.

It was staring back with its hands on its hips.

'Now then,' it said.

The woodsman hesitated. 'I've lost my neighbour's axe,' he said. 'In that pool there. I don't know what I'm going to do now. I can't replace it, and if I don't get these trees felled today, I'll be lucky if I live to regret it. You don't know my master.'

This seemed to amuse the fairy-man.

'Ha! A woodsman with no axe!' it snorted. 'That's a good one. Have you tried fishing it out? It doesn't look like it. You're still dry enough.'

'I can't swim,' the woodsman confessed.

'Interesting. You have a feeble and witless answer for everything I say to you,' the fairy-man said. 'Have you considered a change of profession? The law, perhaps? Or storytelling?'

'I'm no good at anything but cutting down trees,' the woods-man said.

'You're not much good at that by the look of it,' said the fairy-man.

The woodsman looked beseechingly at him.

'Well, you're stuck, then, aren't you?' said the fairy-man. Then he hesitated, and seemed to reconsider. 'Go on, I'll bite, just this once. Where did it fall in?'

'There, in that pool,' the woodsman said.

'Then it'll be that large iron thing that just woke me up,' the fairy-man said. 'Heavy? Sharp? Wedge-shaped? Hole in one end? Painful and dangerous on impact?'

'Yes, that's it!' the woodsman replied. 'Can you get it for me?'

The fairy-man pondered.

'All right,' he said eventually. 'But we have to do this my way. Understand? That's no common or ordinary body of water. You can't just go chucking discarded bits of ironmongery in it. There's a trick to getting these things right.'

The woodsman nodded dumbly.

'I mean it. You have to trust me. No deviating from the plan. Chuck the shaft into the river, and hit the exact spot where the head went in. Do this now.'

Somehow, the woodsman succeeded in hitting the exact spot with the handle.

'Mm, not bad,' said the fairy-man. 'Now, keep your eyes on that spot. Do not take your eyes off that spot. Concentrate. And don't look back, whatever you do. I can't do this stuff with people watching.'

The woodsman did his best to stare at the exact spot on the river's face. He didn't even blink. A terrifying moment passed by. The woodsman wondered if he'd been tricked, but suddenly the water began to bubble, as if the fires of hell were burning beneath the riverbed. The water seethed and turned luminous orange. Leaves lifted off the water, levitating, and spinning anticlockwise. But the woodsman's gaze never flickered.

And then, shaft first, the axe ascended slowly from the water. It looked brand new. It looked better than new: it was suffused by a strange aura and it was newly festooned with mysterious signs and symbols. It floated towards him, as if beckoning him to grasp it.

He grasped it. Strength and vigour seemed to flow into his fingers from the very grain of the wood. He swung the axe, exulting. With a flick of the wrist the tree fell to the earth, then another, and another, until his day's work was done in moments, with scarcely a bead of sweat shed on the earth.

'Behold my gift,' the fairy-man said. 'I suppose you know what this means.'

The woodsman looked up in wonder to meet the gaze of the fairy-man.

'Of course,' he said, smiling. 'It means I can give our Edward his axe back.'

And he marched off home, swinging the axe and singing.

The fairy-man sighed and shrugged, and turned back to the water.

'Bloody Sheffielders,' he muttered, and plummeted back into the deepest reaches of the river, never to be seen again.

Addy 1895: 34–5.

THE BROKEN PITCHER

A girl lived with her mother and sister in a town that lay between two rivers. The girls were known as Lemony and Orangey. Whatever work there was to do in the house, the mother and Lemony would always find a reason why Orangey had to do it. Orangey knew no other treatment and did not protest.

Every morning, the townswomen drew water from the town well in earthen pitchers. Orangey was scarcely taller than the pitchers that were used, so she was always last to arrive at the well and draw water. One morning, she rose as usual before dawn, swept the grate and built the fire, took the earthenware pitcher, and began dragging it towards the well. As she came to the well, she saw the last of the other women hoisting up their pitchers and leaving, spilling drops of water as they went on the glistening cobbles. It was bad luck for her, for if she came to the well in time, she could usually count on help lifting the laden pitcher.

But she came to the well alone, and heaved the pitcher up over the lip of the well, and hooked it to the pulley, and turned the crank, and lowered the pitcher until she heard the splash. Then she waited, and turned the crank again. The pulley line stretched taut. She leaned on the handle with her full weight. Each turn of the crank seemed to add weight to the laden pitcher.

Suddenly the weight got the better of her and she slipped. Her feet scraped and flew, and the crank whipped round with terrible speed. The handle caught her a vicious head-blow.

The pitcher plummeted, and she heard it strike the bottom of the well with an echoing crack and a splash.

For a moment she lay dazed on the ground; then she lifted her head. The air above the town well was shimmering, as if the well was a chimney with a smokeless heat beneath it. Amid the shimmer she thought she saw the form of a woman.

'What are you crying for?'

'I've broken the pitcher,' she said.

'Look', the woman said.

There was a clanking noise, and Orangey looked up to see the crank turning itself. The pitcher appeared at the lip of the well, uncurled its handle, reached up, and unhooked itself from the pulley line. It stood upright for a moment on the lip of the well, and then leaped down. Water splashed from its crown as it ran to stand stiffly beside her, arching its back slightly if it was self-consciously trying to hold a paunch in. It stifled a hiccup.

Orangey scrambled wearily to her feet, and eyed the pitcher warily. It needed no carrying. If she took a step, the pitcher took a step with her, almost too eagerly, as if it wanted her to see that it was making a point of doing everything the same as she did.

They walked home together, hand in hand, and when she came to the doorstep and looked down at the pitcher, its limbs were gone.

It was rocking to and fro slightly under the shifting weight of the water, with the clear liquid still rippling and glistening at its lip. She was quite alone.

Addy 1895: 29–30.

Hob Thrust

There was a shoemaker from Dore who could never earn enough to support his sizeable family. Each day, he would get up at the slit of dawn to make shoes in his cellar beneath his family home. He would stay in his cellar all day, cutting leather, shaping it, stitching it, working furiously hard beneath beads of sweat to keep a one-man assembly line going. He would scarcely see daylight for fear of starvation. He would even work at weekends, missing church; the fear of his deprived family's health outweighed his fear of God's wrath. And each year, money would get tighter and tighter, and the shoemaker and his family would get poorer and poorer.

This upset him very much. He had never known any other life beyond making shoes, as his father had taught him, and he had become as good a shoemaker as his father was – perhaps even better – but as good a salesman? That, sadly, he had never achieved. And as the years went by his fingers got slower and slower, and his eyes grew dimmer and dimmer.

One day, the shoemaker felt tired earlier than usual. He tried to fight the feeling off, but it overpowered him. He knew he had to go for a little lie-down. So he left the cellar early, with a fresh piece of leather still on his workbench. As a joke, he called out to his bench, 'You'll have to do this one without me.'

Then he shut the door with a loud slam.

The shoemaker went for a little lie-down, and at once fell into a deep sleep that lasted well into the next morning. He woke late in the morning, feeling guilty and befuddled, and ran down to the cellar without pausing for even a late bite of breakfast. When he opened the door, everything was as he had left it, ready for him to start work, except one small detail.

A pair of shoes.

A freshly made pair of ladies' red lace-up boots sat on the table where he had left the leather.

The shoemaker stared at the boots with very mixed emotions. He paced round them, studying them closely, taking care not to touch them. Even his expert eye could detect no flaw. Each shoe was immaculately made and exactly matched to the other in every single detail. Together, they were perfection.

Excited, he grabbed the boots, and rushed upstairs.

He did not even bother to tell his wife, but simply grabbed his coat from the banister, and cycled to town to sell the boots. Almost at once, a rich-looking fellow stopped his driver and summoned the shoemaker to bring his wares for inspection. Once the red lace-up boots had been seen, money had hardly even been discussed; a fat bag of coins had been slapped in the shoemaker's hand, and the rich man had nodded to his driver and hared off with another present for his wife. In five minutes, the shoemaker had made more money than he had turned over the whole preceding month.

The shoemaker stared at the money, all thought of boots banished from his mind. The things he thought of buying! A joint of lamb. Potatoes and greens. New clothes. A long list of luxuries. He even considered paying some bills. But there was a feeling deep in his gut that prevented him. He owed it to himself to use this gift wisely. He knew it was his last chance at success.

He bought enough leather to make two pairs of shoes, and then he went straight home.

The next night, the shoemaker left the fresh leather on the bench, and went straight to bed. As he had the night before, he overslept, skipped breakfast, and ran down to his workshop in the cellar.

Everything was as he had left it, ready for him to start work, except for one small detail.

Two pairs of shoes: ladies' court shoes, in snowy white.

They were better than the red boots – better shoes, in fact, than the shoemaker had ever seen in all his long working life. He didn't even shut the door properly on his way out; he simply took both pairs of shoes, and sold them. At this rate, he thought, he would have enough to lift his family out of poverty. The things he could buy! The luxuries that awaited him …!

But no. He felt something deep inside. His gut was telling him to use this gift wisely, so he went back and bought more leather – enough for four pairs of shoes – which he took straight home.

There followed the same routine as on the previous two nights; and the next night it was the same, and the next. Each night the shoemaker went to bed early, rose late, skipped breakfast, and went straight to the cellar. And the result was four perfect pairs of new shoes, and then eight pairs, and then sixteen.

The shoemaker could hardly spend his money quick enough. Each morning, he would get up, and go downstairs to find more and more shoes, each better than the last batch.

After a while, the shoemaker realised that he could afford to have the leather delivered to him in bulk. He ordered a huge batch of leather, took delivery, carried it down to the cellar, left it on the bench, and went off to pay a visit to the pub – a luxury he could now afford.

As he sat and nursed his pint, contemplating early retirement and a life of ease and leisure, it occurred to him for the first time to wonder who – or what – was making the shoes, and, more to the point – as he explained to the landlord – what could be done to thank him – or it – in person.

'So you're telling me that you do the same thing every night?' the landlord demanded. 'You just put the leather on the table, and go to bed early, and the next day someone's done all the hard work for you?'

The shoemaker nodded. 'Someone or some*thing*,' he said. 'It's been like that for weeks.'

'And you've no idea what's behind it?'

'None,' the shoemaker said, and sipped his pint.

'Well, you know what you need to do, don't you?' the landlord said.

The shoemaker looked at him quizzically.

'Go down in the middle of the night. When he least expects it,' the landlord said. 'Around three o'clock, when it's pitch black.'

The shoemaker thought well of the landlord's suggestion, so he refrained from drinking a skinful in case the beer put him to sleep, and then went home to sit up and watch.

Three o'clock came, and down to the cellar on silent tiptoes the shoemaker crept. As he approached he could hear someone at work, and see shadows flickering in the candlelight.

And he peered very slowly and carefully around the door.

It was a little man.

A very hairy little man.

He was so hairy, in fact, that some might have said that he looked like a bit of a hob.

And the shoemaker then realised who it was. Hob Thrust himself.

The mountainous consignment of fresh leather on the bench before him was dwindling rapidly – indeed, visibly, for never had the shoemaker seen any man or woman, hob or human, work half as fast or half as well as Hob Thrust worked, whizzing back and forth from bench to cupboard, crafting shoes at lightning speeds. There were shoes everywhere: men's boots, women's shoes, brogues and sandals and shoes of all kinds and colours and sizes, finished and half-finished, stacked neatly in the corners, spilling over every available surface and lying on the floor in untidy heaps. The cupboards were spilling open. The floor was invisible. The whole cellar was on the point of drowning in shoes.

In panic, the shoemaker grabbed arms full of shoes and ran up into his house, to store them anywhere they would go. He crammed the shoes into corners and cupboards and under shelves. Then he ran downstairs to the cellar again, and back up with another armful of shoes, and down again, and up again, and down and up again, and again and again. Every time he went back down into the cellar, the mountain of leather was a little smaller and Hob Thrust had made more and more shoes. Within an hour the whole house was filled: the kitchen, the living room, even the children's bedrooms had become storerooms for shoes.

Hob Thrust was still going to work and he didn't stop. As the cellar filled, Hob had resorted to tossing them up the stairs into the kitchen, where the shoemaker would rush halfway down the stairs to catch them.

In the end, the shoemaker had to open a window, and was running back and forth between the cellar and the window at full speed, tossing the shoes out of the window into the street as fast as Hob Thrust could make them. And anyone who walked past the shoemaker's that night, or the next morning, would have thought that the finest shoes that ever shod a foot had been falling from the sky, as plentifully and cheaply as flakes of snow.

There is an old saying in Sheffield that relates to this story, back when the little mesters were crafting knives in their rented workshop areas in the Sheffield steel factories. When a knife maker would boast about how many knives they had made that day, the popular retort was: 'Ah, tha can mak em faster than Hob Thrust can throw shoes out o t window!' And any knife-maker who heard that would know that his leg was being pulled, for never could any man or woman work half as fast or so well as Hob Thrust.

This tale comes from Dore. It is – of course – the same basic type as the famous tale of the Elves and the Shoemaker, the first item in 'The Elves' ('Die Wichtelmänner'), which is no. 39 in the famous Children's and Household Tales of the Brothers Grimm *(1857 edition). The Grimms first printed this story in German in 1812, but there was a steady stream of translations from the Grimms' tales into English throughout the nineteenth century, and the tale of the Elves and the Shoemaker was one of the first reproduced in English, in 1823. It had thus been a mainstay of vernacular English literature for a whole lifetime by the time Addy collected this story, around 1890.*

Given this dating, the tale of Hob Thrust and the shoemaker of Dore might easily be a straight borrowing from the Grimms, but Addy's story has enough local connections to suggest that it may derive, at least partly, from an independent tradition. Hob is a standard term in northern English for an elf or supernatural being, and Hob Thrust (Hurst, etc.) is a common name for a number of individual beings, including several

*associated with prehistoric burial mounds, such as an Obtrusch Roque
near Kirkbymoorside on the North York Moors (which, shorn of its
fake-exotic spelling, is probably just Hob Thrust's Rock). Accordingly,
on Beeley Moor near Bakewell in Derbyshire, not far from the setting
of Addy's tale of Hob Thrust and the shoemaker, is Hob Hurst's House,
a rare rectangular Bronze Age burial mound, crudely excavated in 1853
and now in fairly decayed condition, but still easily found.*

Addy 1895: 39–40.

THE CARD PLAYER AND THE DEVIL

The cards were down on the table and the message was clear: pictures, numbers, spades and clubs, diamonds and hearts … and you lose. No matter what the rules of the game, you lose.

The young man was a sore loser. His older workmates were sore winners, especially when a whole week's earnings were chanced on a single hand. The young man had gone all in, and out the doors he went with dry, empty pockets. Just before he left the door, he turned back to his gloating friends, their eyes squinting and their faces messy with coal.

'Sod you all!' he declared. 'You must have been cheating.'

Laughter followed, a good two minutes' laughter, with glasses raised in mock toast.

'You were in it together!' he shouted. 'You must have been! Too often for one night. There's no way.'

'It must have been down to luck, then,' one of his pals snapped back. 'You know it yourself. Chance makes every man a loser, sooner or later. It was only a matter of time before we got you back.'

'Rubbish!' the young man spat as he stamped his foot. 'Sod you all! If you're going to cheat, I might as well play with the Devil himself.'

Everyone went quiet.

The young man barely noticed. Half drunk, he hit the cobbled path and made his way homeward. Down the long lane he went towards the woods near Totley. It was cold, and a sober man would have had to have been brave to walk alone on a night like that. The moon was hidden behind thick clouds, and the fog seemed to follow him even into the woods, but not a single person did he meet on his way.

The young man pressed on in thick darkness. He had even gambled his matches.

The woods were eerie as woods are in the dead of night. The trees ruffled their leaves in the wind, but there were no signs of wildlife, nor sound from man or beast.

There was a sound though, just behind him. Like claws against marble. He turned around quick to find – nothing. He narrowed his eyes, trying to focus. Somewhere ahead of him there seemed to be a strange black figure. He couldn't quite fix his eyes on it.

The sound came again, directly behind him. He span around to find – nothing. Again.

The wind died down. The trees went still. The sound came again, this time to his right. He turned. There was nothing to his right, but when he veered slowly to his left, he saw … something …

He turned to see the Devil himself.

For he hadn't realised where he was until it was too late. The Devil walks in straight lines, true, and what better place to find him than at a crossroads?

The Devil was scary enough, but he didn't look like the vicar had described him. He looked like a man like any other. But he wore a lot of black: a long coat and hat, doubtless intended to cover any stray horns. The eyes were different though. Glowing red. Windows to the soul, the young man had once heard someone say – in every case except this.

The Devil smiled at the petrified young man.

'I heard you wanted to play some cards with me,' the Devil said. 'Well, here I am.'

The Devil snapped his fingers expertly, in spite of his long, immaculately manicured fingernails. In the dead centre of the crossroads, two chairs and a table appeared. The young man found himself sat on one of those chairs.

'Mind if I deal?' the Devil smirked.

'I have nothing to play with,' the young man said.

'Sure you do,' the Devil replied. 'You just haven't played for it before.'

The young man blinked. Clueless.

'Very valuable to me; not so much to you. I'm sure we can find you something of value if you do win. That money you lost, maybe.'

'What do you want from me?' the young man quavered.

'Your soul …'

And that was that. The young man jumped out of his chair and began to sprint in the other direction. He ran through the woods as fast as he could, until he came to some crossroads.

There was the Devil again at the next crossroads, waiting for him, asking him, 'Are you ready to play?'

The young man ran in another direction, sprinting as fast as he could, through the woods for a good mile … the woods seemed bigger than usual; bigger than the young man remembered. He came to another crossroads.

'You said it in the tavern. You would rather play with me. Have you changed your mind or something?'

The young man ran again one final time, his heart pounding in his chest, his brain reeling for want of air, two miles straight through woodland, until he came to another crossroads. There stood the Devil again.

'Don't you see? You cannot beat me,' the Devil said.

The young man fell to his knees.

'Are you ready to gamble?'

'No!'

The young man closed his eyes and concentrated hard. He did something he hadn't done for years. He prayed.

Suddenly, all the natural sounds of the woods came back. The wind picked up. The wild animals of the forest began to move. Normally such things would have filled the young man with fear, but now it all filled him with relief. He opened his eyes and the Devil was gone.

He never gambled again.

Addy 1895: 41.

SIMMERDALE

Semerwater lies in Raydale. Legend tells that a village of one long street used to stand where the lake now lies. Its name was Simmerdale. The church stood at one end of the village. At the far end, a little apart from the other houses, stood the cottage of the one villager who never went to church, an old woman, last of one of the old Quaker families who had been busy in the northern dales around Sedbergh ever since the Commonwealth days.

Late one evening, an old beggar woman from far away came on foot over the brow, and saw the village of Simmerdale spread out below her. She had barely a penny in her pocket, and had had little enough to eat or drink all day, and nothing but the sky to cover her, so she was glad enough to see the village, thinking that she could beg a cup of milk and a porch to sit in to keep the worst of the night's cold off.

She gazed at the long, narrow village street, with the church at the northern end, and reckoned that her best chances of charity lay with the churchgoers, and the churchgoers would naturally live close to the church.

So when she came to the village, she stepped up to the house nearest the church, and was promptly sent away by the wife of the house, with a harsh word.

She tried the next house, and it was just as bad. The next house brought no better luck, nor the next, and she tried every house in the village without luck, until there was nowhere left to go but the old Quaker woman's cottage.

She rattled at the latch, and the old woman answered, and gave her hot milk and porridge, and offered her a place by the hearth to pass the night.

But the old woman remained sitting in the porch of the cottage, drinking the milk, and when she had finished it, she rose to her feet, and looked back over the village where every house had turned her away. She lifted her hand, and said in a quiet but piercing voice:

> Simmerdale, Simmerdale, Simmerdale, sink,
> Except for the Quaker who gave me a drink.

And when morning came, the old woman was gone, and the village was gone, and the lake of Semerwater lay where it had once stood; but the old Quaker woman lived on in her cottage on the margins of the lake.

Raydale is off Upper Wensleydale, south of Bainbridge, and Semerwater is a natural lake – a rare thing in the Yorkshire Dales. 'Semer' rhymes with 'dilemma'. Addy obtained this story from 'a native of the North Riding now resident in Sheffield' – one of many immigrants into the burgeoning city. The story exists in numerous versions, and was in circulation by the 1850s. In some, the traveller was not a beggar but St Paul, or Jesus, or Joseph of Arimathea, and the charity came from a poor old couple. Raydale is rich in evidence of prehistoric and Roman settlement, and possibly a glimpse of old dwelling-places inspired the story of a drowned village. The Quaker movement began in and around nearby Sedbergh in the early 1650s, and there is an old Quaker Meeting House in Raydale, at Countersett, which does indeed stand at the opposite end of the lake from the site of the church at Stalling Busk. We have gratefully relied on information from the Raydale Project, available through Tourist Information at Hawes.

Addy 1895: 61; Westwood and Simpson 2006 (2005): 835–38.

8

'LIGHTEN I' THE MORNING': SOUTH YORKSHIRE LIFE

LAUGHTON-EN-LE-MORTHEN

Every one passing through the neighbourhood … will have admired the beautiful church spire of Laughton-en-le-Morthen which is visible for many miles round, and, from its elevated position and graceful proportions, may justly be regarded as an ornament to the whole surrounded district. The inhabitants call it 'Lighten i' the Morning' for, say they, 'the first beams of the rising sun play around the vane at the top of the spire like lightning'.

Laughton-en-le-Morthen does, in fact, seem to be named 'Leighton in the mornyng' on John Speed's 1610 map of the West Riding. Having arrived just in time to photograph the spire catching the rays of the sunlight of Sunday, 5 October 2014, we can state with eyewitness confidence that it is indeed an arresting and very beautiful sight.

Tomlinson 1860: 95; '1610 Map of West Riding, by John Speed', www.rotherhamweb.co.uk/h/map/speed1610.htm, accessed 4-1-2015.

THE SWALLOW'S NEST

The first building on the site of the future village of Swallownest was an inn. It was built in the years around 1770 by one Jonathan Swallow, of Chesterfield, on the 'handkerchief piece', a (presumably small) plot of land at the crossroads. As he was working, a friend happened to pass by and remark, 'Well, Mr Swallow, you're building yourself a nest!' The name stuck to the house, as it stuck to the village that eventually grew up about it.

The village (Swallow Nest on some old maps, still upheld as the correct spelling by some) grew up in the early 1800s, around a toll bar and public house of the same name, listed as such in White's Directory of 1833. The Swallow Nest Inn is marked on one 1855 map (in the possession of the Family History Journal*), at a point then on the open road, but now on the western edge of the centre of the greatly enlarged village, where four roads meet: Rotherham Road, Chesterfield Road, Main Street and Park Hill. The pub on this crossroads was more recently named the Wetherby: it stands high on a fairly steep hillside, with extensive views of the area, a location which may add point to the name, given that swallows nest at the top of walls. The story was recounted in 1967 by Mrs J. Knowles (b. 1889), in these terms:*

A rider going through this small hamlet one day saw a man called Swallow up a ladder building what appeared to be a small cottage. The rider said to him, 'Hello, Mr Swallow, are you building yourself a nest?' The old man replied, 'That is just what I am doing,' hence the name 'Swallow Nest'.

Jonathan Swallow's daughter Elizabeth married a John Ward, and the Wards were innkeepers at Swallownest thereafter. Elizabeth's grandson John was still an innkeeper in the village in the 1830s. His wife converted to Methodism and founded the first congregation, in what became a thriving Methodist tradition in the village, in the very kitchen of her husband's equally thriving public house. The domestic friction generated by this strikingly awkward arrangement was still spoken of in Swallownest as late as 1967; Ward's habit was seemingly to tolerate the preaching of his wife's guests until explicit mention was made of the Devil or hell, at which point he would strike the floor and bluntly interject, 'That's enough!' This cannot have endeared him to the Methodists if they were typical of the preachers of the region – one of whom was once said to have hanged his cat for mousing on the Sabbath. Work on the first Methodist chapel at Swallownest began in 1847.

Swallownest

The site of the village of Swallownest has been suggested by local histori-
ans as a possible site of the Battle of Brunanburh (see Chapter 1).

Rotherham Advertiser 9-7-1938, 15-7-1967 (RALS); *Rotherham*
Circuit Magazine, April–June 1968 (RALS); 'Swallownest,
Yorkshire, 1855', www.familyhistoryjournal.com/data/maps/
map-large-swallownest.html, accessed 9-9-2013.

HELL HOLE, WHISTON MEADOWS

Hell Hole was the startling name for the 'old cut', an artificial channel
in the brook near the mill in Whiston Meadows, remembered by
Rotherham author Gervase Phinn (2010) as 'a dark and sinister stretch
of water'. The following story was written by 'Old Whistonian' in 1950.

I remember an old farmer who had a labourer who was mentally
deficient. One day a horse named 'Boxer' was found in the 'old cut'
near these old houses up to its belly in mud. It was got out with
some difficulty. Some few days later another horse got in, and while
they were getting it out the farmer was heard to exclaim: 'What a
hell hole.' Later still, 'Boxer' was found in the same predicament,
by the labourer referred to above, and he went back to the farm and
told his employer: 'Owd Boxer's in t hell hoil again.'

'Where is t hell hole, Billy?' was the query.

'Why, yer ruddy fool,' was the reply, 'didn't *you* call it hell hoil?'

Rotherham Advertiser 18-2-1950 (RALS); 'Hell hole, Whiston
Meadows, Whiston 1910–1915', www.scran.ac.uk/database/
record.php?usi=000-000-678-412-C, accessed 6-9-2013.

THE NATIVES OF WHISTON

A song about the natives of Whiston, *c.* 1900. Contributed to the
Whiston Parish Magazine in 1982 by local historian C.H. Walker,

and published in David Pike's feature 'Whiston Scene'. We have
cut some apostrophes, but otherwise reproduced the lyric exactly.
'Barm' is yeast – as a boy in Chesterfield, Dave Eyre, now of
Sheffield, recalls being sent for a 'pennorth o barm'. The dig at
Timothy Elliott shows that the dialect *eɪ* diphthong for standard
English *aɪ* or *iː* was alive and kicking, furnishing a 'meat/weight'
rhyme which you can't get in standard English. With references to
the village blacksmith, beehive-maker, cobbler, and roadmender –
this vivid lyric argues for a high degree of self-sufficiency.

> At bottom o town the row begins,
> Owd lass Pilley taks lodgers in;

> *Tit fer lar lar alay*
> *Wack fer lar a laddy ho!*

> Owd George Walker's a cobbler be trade,
> En his son - - 's a roving blade;
> Mary Yeardley she sells flowers,
> En when it - - s owd Tommy looks sour;
> Dinna Roddy she sells barm,
> Henry Ellam will do yer no harm;
> Fanny Linnet she sells bread,
> Martha and Bill Ogden's allas e bed;
> Aaron Roddy he keeps dogs,
> Danny Weldon's surrounded bi bogs;
> Mister Moss he's up to t mark,
> He works his men til neight gits dark;
> Timothy Elliott he sells meight,
> If yo don't watch him e'll ge yo short weight;
> Mister Martin's getten the gout,
> Mary Roddis's allas out;
> Johnny Bagshaw he keeps t Ball,
> Benny Hammond's thin an tall;
> Jossy Armitage he feeds pigs,
> At Mister Clay's yo can buy some figs;

Johnny Menchin maks bee hives,
William Woodhead he's had three wives;
Owd John - - he sells beer,
Henry White he looks so queer;
Owd George Corker works on t roads,
Johnny Turner's a drunken owd toad;
T village blacksmith's William Street,
Poor John Bassendate's bad on his feet;
At Sitwell Arms lives Mary Foers,
She chalks yer slate on t back o t doors;
Thomas Parkin will kill you a pig,
Mark Belk'll dance you a gig.

Hey up, hey up, owd Charley Ward,
He's heading turnips out in t yard.
If we catch him we will bash him,
Hey up, hey up, owd Charley Ward.

Whiston Parish Magazine, January–March 1982 (RALS).

WILLIAM LEE OF SHEFFIELD

William Lee, who lived in the High Street in the eighteenth century, was a well-known gambler and a very regular frequenter of the Bay Childers public house.

Naturally Lee made a point of attending all the local races and one day, on his way to Doncaster, he noticed the coach in front swaying very violently.

This coach was carrying Lee's wife and only son, but … Lee shouted to his friend sitting beside him, 'Five to four that carriage turns over and our John is killed!'

Vickers 1973. Quoted word for word.

BLIND STEPHEN

The writer Henry Mayhew observed that there were two kinds of street fiddler in Victorian cities: skilled ones, and blind ones.

Mayhew might have added that the blind fiddlers were not always so blind, since street music – one of the few paid occupations open to the blind – was often little more than begging, and many a beggar feigned blindness in order to do it.

Mayhew was writing about London. It was a different matter in Sheffield, where the blind fiddlers were trained musicians, respected practitioners of a recognised craft. This was largely thanks to Samuel Goodlad, an excellent musician and teacher, and landlord of the Q in the Corner on Paradise Square, where Sheffield spread back – through narrow cobbled streets and clustered inns and offices and houses and churches – up the steep hill behind the castle above the river.

Samuel Goodlad was not above pride in his musicianship, and if there was a new tune in vogue, Goodlad had to be the first and only fiddler in Sheffield to know how to play it. Among the greatest of the blind fiddlers of old Sheffield was Blind Stephen, and Goodlad would be particularly careful never to play his new tunes if he knew Blind Stephen was in earshot, since Blind Stephen, as he knew, could learn a tune at a single hearing.

So fierce was the competition between the two men that once, not long after Samuel Goodlad's wedding, Blind Stephen once had himself smuggled into the Q in the Corner in a sack, just so that he could hear Goodlad's new tune. Stephen's friends asked for the

tune, and heard it, and then carried the sack out, before returning to the pub. A little later that night, of course, Blind Stephen appeared at the Q in the Corner, and the same group of friends pointedly asked him if he could play that tune that Samuel Goodlad was forever boasting about.

The Q in the Corner (now offices), Sheffield

'Better than anyone in town,' Blind Stephen replied, loud enough for Goodlad to overhear it. Goodlad then angrily bet Stephen a leg of mutton with all the trimmings that he could not play the tune. Stephen won the bet, and sat down to his mutton. When he left the pub, much later, he asked the landlady (the newly wed Mrs Goodlad) for the loan of a lantern – for the streets on his way home, he said, promising to return it the next day.

The request was made so easily and naturally that Mrs Goodlad lent the lantern without a thought. Blind Stephen left the inn and set off for Pinstone Lane, cutting a quaint figure, with the lantern burning brightly, held aloft in one hand, and his fiddle tucked under the other arm.

'And what use is a lantern to a blind man?' one of the regulars asked.

Mrs Goodlad hastily sent a serving girl off to retrieve the lantern, but Blind Stephen refused to give it up.

'It's late,' he explained, 'and the streets are dark. Full of drunks reeling around on their way home,' he added.

'So?' the girl demanded. 'Could you not see your way home in the dark, then?'

'Does think I borrowed it for me sen?' Blind Stephen demanded. 'If anyone knocked me down and smashed my fiddle, I should be ruined. I can't see it, but others can.'

The extraordinary story of the Sheffield Blind Fiddlers – who formed, mainly under Goodlad's influence, an organised class of respected professional musicians, with regular fixtures in Sheffield streets and concerts in the years around 1810 – is told by Paul Davenport in his book Total Eclipse. *Goodlad's inn, the Q in the Corner, occupied a double lot in the south-west corner of Paradise Square; Blind Stephen lived not far away, on Pinstone Street. Stephen and Goodlad were both active in Sheffield toward the end of the eighteenth century – that is, in the heyday of radical Sheffield.*

Small in stature and fierce in temperament, Blind Stephen was not the only blind fiddler remembered for his pithy sayings. J. Edward Vickers reports that another, Blind John, would busk hymns around Savile Street and Attercliffe Road, and would stop to ask his wife,

'Is anybody about?' If there wasn't, he would say gloomily, 'Come along then. We can sing "Come to Jesus" till Hell fetches us, but if there's nob'dy about, nob'dy'll gie us owt.'

After a long campaign, the memory of the Blind Fiddlers was finally enshrined in a plaque on the wall of the old Q in the Corner, in 2014.

Vickers 1973; Cf. 'The Blind Fiddlers',
www.hallamtrads.co.uk/BlindF.html, accessed 10-1-2015.

TOMMY TAYLOR OF KIMBERWORTH

In 1955, W.F. Smith of Kimberworth recorded anecdotes of town characters, which he dated to the years around 1900.

Tommy Taylor the gravedigger was hard of hearing; no matter how loudly he was asked whose grave he was digging, he might easily reply 'Nine foot!' but a whispered offer to stand him a pint in the Travellers' Inn would meet with the immediate reply that 'he'd be there in a minute'. Tommy once complained that he had dug a grave so deep he had had to go and fetch himself a ladder to get out of it.

Around the same time, Ted Bush had a cobbler's shop, which was also a centre for village gossip and a place to meet and kill time. The shop had a special chair reserved for strangers and newcomers, who, after sitting for a while, would 'jump up in a hurry' – the chair was fitted with a mechanical device which caused a needle to stab upwards from the middle of the seat.

Rotherham Advertiser 12-3-1955 (RALS).

ARON ALLOTT OF THORPE HESLEY

In the early 1900s Aron Allott was landlord of the Gate Inn at Thorpe Hesley. The inn-sign bore a famous legend:

This gate hangs well
And hinders none
Refresh and pay
And then pass on

In 1915 the inn was forced to close, seemingly owing to the war government's notorious restrictions on alcohol consumption (commemorated in Weston and Lee's hit 1917 song, 'Lloyd George's Beer'). Allott is said to have sent the famous inn sign to Lloyd George himself in protest. This story may have gathered scale in the telling, since some early versions of the story report only that Allott threatened to do so.

Chessman, n.d.: 65 (RALS); *Rotherham Advertiser* 27-8-1910
[N.B. date from handwritten note in margin] (RALS);
Rotherham Annual 1915 (RALS); 'Vintage Audio: Lloyd George's Beer',
www.firstworldwar.com/audio/lloydgeorgesbeer.html, accessed 6-9-2013.

THE VICAR OF CAWTHORNE

The vicar's stipend at Cawthorne used to be so low that vicars often had to take work in order to make up a living wage. One vicar worked as a basket-maker. Every week, with clockwork regularity, he would start on Monday, making a basket a day, and when he had six baskets made he would know it was Saturday and would lay his baskets aside and prepare for the Sunday services.

One Sunday in church, the parish was assembled and the congregation waiting, and the hour for service to begin came and went. Still the vicar did not appear. After a time, a few of the parishioners made their way to the vicarage to find the vicar working on his Saturday basket. He had been to Sheffield Fair on the Tuesday and forgotten that he had failed to get round to making the Tuesday basket. He had been reckoning time by his total of baskets as usual, [and] was most surprised and disconcerted to learn that it was Sunday already.

Pratt 1882. Quoted word for word.

BETTY OF DORE

One wet Monday morning in the 1800s, an old woman who lived just outside the village of Dore passed down the village street. She was obviously dressed in her best clothes, with pattens on her feet and she proudly carried her one and only umbrella.

The village schoolmistress happened to be standing at the door of the school, which was also her cottage, and she was extremely surprised to see Betty at such an unusual time. So she called, 'Betty, where are you going?'

'I'm for the chapel,' answered Betty, surprised at being questioned.

'Ah, going to be married?' asked the schoolmistress, with a broad smile.

'Noo!' was Betty's response.

'What then?' was the next question.

'What do we go every Sunday for?' Betty replied.

A look of amazement came over the schoolteacher's face. 'Sunday! But it's Monday today!' she exclaimed.

'The ferrits it is!' grumbled Betty. Then realisation dawned, 'Then it's the old whatcake [oatcake] what's done it!'

'But how's that?' asked the schoolmistress.

'Why,' responded Betty, 'I always bake a peck of meal and it just serves me a week, but it happened to make two cakes more this time and that's what's driven me into Monday. What makes it worse,' continued the old woman, apparently horrified at breaking the Sabbath, 'I was white-washing yesterday!'

Vickers 1973. Quoted word for word.

TWO–NOWT

There was a husband who just could not stand being henpecked any longer. He decided that he had to leave, so he went off, telling his wife, 'Ah'm barn t cup final.'

He could not stay away long; three years later he was back again. As he walked in she asked him, 'Well, what's tha got to say for thi sen?'

'Won. Two–nowt,' he said.

She replied, 'All reight then, get thi coit off, an sit thissen darn, but doon't blame me if thi tea's cowd.'

Chessman n.d.: 20 (RALS). Quoted word for word.

Martha and Albert

Albert was sixty-five and they sacked him at the pit where he had worked since he was a lad. They told him he was too old, but he'd have his pension.

'Pension, pension,' he said to Martha when he got home, 'what good's b– pension? It won't keep me in beer and bacca.'

'Nay, Albert lad, dooant take on sooer,' said Martha, 'wis'll be all reight, thee come inta t front room, I've a surprise fa thee.'

They go into the front room and Martha says, 'Tha sees them three cottages across t rooad, next ta t pub on t corner?'

'Ah, I owt to do, ah seed em ivery day as ah wor barn t pit,' said Albert.

'Well, Albert lad, them three cottages is ah cottages, they belong ta thee and me. Bit a rent'll help us art nah tha's gien up warkin.'

'What's tha mean, Martha, them's ah cottages? Ah's that come abart?'

'Well, Albert lad, it waar like this here. When thee and me got wed, ah sed to missen: ivery time tha make love ta mi, ah'd put orf a crarn away. After t twelve months ah'd managed ta buy t first cottage. Ten years later ah bowt second un, and that knows we've been wed nigh on fotty year, ah've just managed to buy t last un, so tha sees, wis'll be all reight.'

'Martha las,' said Albert, right taken aback, 'Martha las, I do wish tha'd ah told mi. If ah'd nobbut known, ah'd niver have laiked away; why, we cood ah ad t pub on t corner an all!'

Chessman n.d.: 21 (RALS). Quoted word for word.

GORGONZOLA

At a farmer's dinner a veteran Thorper was given a piece of gorgon-
zola cheese. He had never seen this sort before, and after being told
it was not mouldy, but made like that, he popped a piece in his
mouth. A few minutes later he spit it out, pulling a long face.

'Haven't you ever tasted it before?' he was asked. 'No, ah've niver
tasted it afore, but ah've often trud in it.'

Chessman n.d.: 21 (RALS). Quoted word for word.

POTATOES

A lady in the greengrocer's shop, watching the grocer shovelling potatoes into her bag, said, 'Don't give me all that muck in t bottom.'

'Ah'm not givin it yer, love,' he replied, 'Ah'm sellin it yer.'

Chessman, n.d.: 29A (RALS). Quoted word for word.

THE GROCERY TRADE

People are always glad of an excuse to complain about things, such
as the two local shopkeepers who were overheard to say: 'Things
are war [worse] now na than they war when t war was on. Even folk
who don't pay aren't orderin owt.'

Chessman, n.d.: 29A (RALS). Quoted word for word.

PICKLING IN THORNE

There is the story of the Thorne woman who, one rainy day, called into the grocer's shop for a pound of onions. 'Are you pickling missus?' asked the grocer. 'No, you daft thing,' she said, 'it's running off mi rain coit.'

Chessman, n.d.: 20 (RALS). Quoted word for word.

SIMMIE AND THE CART

This story, of a prank played on a salt-and-sawdust seller, was told in the 1930s to the countryside writer Robert Bielby, by a man whose name Bielby does not record, when they met by chance on Cortworth Lane, Wentworth, making for Rotherham on foot. The storyteller, as he said, was '"Romish'"[i.e., Rawmarsh] bred an born'. The prank had been played in Rawmarsh years before. We have removed the apostrophes, which Bielby used freely in his dialect spellings, but otherwise this is the story exactly as Bielby wrote it up.

Owd Simmie wer used to cummin rahnd eerie Fridi wi sawdust and salt, an allus left is donkey and cart at t end o ohr street, while e went rahnd for orders. At one o t street ends there wer a grass field, an one day we tuk t donkey aat while he wor away and led it into t field. We then gor owd o t cart and shuvved t shafts throo t edge [hedge] and backed t donkey in to em an geared im up as e wor afore. Then we iddied ahr sels in an entry [hid in a gateway] across t road and waited till t owd man cum back. Well, nah, when e seed t donkey in t field and t cart on t road e wor nocked aat, and stood like a cloas poast [clothes post] tryin to reckon up ah this thing ed appened.

Then t bobby cum up an wanted to kno what Simmie meant wi eving t cart on t road an t donkey in t field, but, ov course, Simmie cuddent tell im owt abaat it.

But as e were a good natured bobby e elped t owd man to get things reight ageean while t lads ed a reight good laff an enjoyed eerie minute on it. When all wer put reight, t bobby pulled aat is pocket book an put summat dahn in it. We were all a bit sceered at what wud appen if e fun aat who ed been in at this joke, so non on us darrent split on each other, an Simmie never fun aat who ed been in at this bit o crosswork. That wor nearest at ave iver been to t police court.

Rotherham Advertiser, 16-5-1936 (RALS); Acknowledgements to Chris Coates and Jim White.

THE KILKENNY DEVIL

This story was told some time before 1860 to John Tomlinson, over the course of a walk near Doncaster. The storyteller and his listener were both Irish labourers. Storytelling was clearly a normal way of shortening long journeys on foot and immigrants to modern South Yorkshire have often brought their own stories to throw into the mix. This is the story word for word as Tomlinson writes it, but we have edited his dialect spelling.

'I'll tell you a true story which happened to Mike Gallagher.'

'Did you know Mike?' enquired the other Irishman.

'No, but Patrick Doherty came from the same county, and he heard aal about it at Kilkenny.'

'Oo, aa,' said his companion.

'Mike Gallagher was once decently off; he had a fine stock o cows, but disease got among em, and they fell down like rotten praties. He had only one left, and he must sell it to pay the rent. When he had driv it ta the fair, as he was travelling, he met a gentleman in black, and he thought it was His Reverence [i.e., the Devil], and the gentleman says, says he, "My man, how much for that cow?"

'"Five pounds for the cow," says Mike, "and it's cheap."

'"I'll have it," says he, and the money was paid. "It's the last cow you've got," says he.

'"Sure Your Reverence is right," says Mike, "and it's like parting with the last drop o my blood."

'"I fancy you would like the cow back again," says he.

'"True enough I should like her back, for it's my only beast – I want the cow and want the money too."

'"You'd like em both back," said the gentleman.

'"Faith, and Your Reverence is right there," says Mike.

'"I'll give you cow, and money, and all," says he, "if you'll consent to one thing."

'"I'll sure enough consent. What is it, Your Reverence?"

'"Tis an easy thing," says he, and he whispered – "I only want a drop o your blood."

'So he let him bleed him. You need not laugh, sir,' said the narrator.

'Indeed, it's all true!' replied the other man.

'Mike driv his cow and money both home, and got as rich as a middleman. His praties grew into sovereigns by the bushel.'

'Indeed, it's all true!' exclaimed his companion. 'What happened to Mike now?'

'His mind got uneasy, and he went to Father Jarratt, and Father Jarratt said, "Mike," says he, "how is it you are so rich?"

'"Why, saving Your Reverence, since I met that gentleman in black."

'"What's that you're talking about a gentleman in black?" asked the priest.

'So Mike made a clane breast. Father Jarratt shook his head.

'"It's a sad job," said he, "Why, you've sold yourself to the Devil, and he's your blood to testify." The priest tried to raise him but he couldn't.'

'Couldn't he though?' enquired the other.

'He couldn't, and the man was near distracted. At last there came a holy young man from college determined to do something for him, so he gets him upstairs, and by the shinbone of Saint Clement didn't they say some Ave Marias, but the Devil a bit would he come for a long time. But just as the clock struck twelve, up he came, and, says he, "Bad luck to you! What are you making all this to-do for? The man is mine body and soul," says he. Mike's sister, hearing such a noise, came in with a candle, and they saw the Devil caper-ing about the room in the shape of an eel. At last he jumps into the poor lassie's mouth and went down her throat.'

'Bedad, and that was quare now!' exclaimed the other Irishman.

'He soon had to flit from the lassie, and disappeared in a flame of fire, taking part of the cabin roof with him. People came all round the county to see the house.'

'And what got Mike's money?' enquired the other, 'And what become of himself after?'

'It melted away like wax, and he had to do penance all his life; and he was never to eat twice in the same place, nor wear a hat as long as he lived.'

Tomlinson 1860: 113–14.

Nesbitt and the Snowman

Dave Eyre of Sheffield was the first to tell us the widely known story of the snowman in the Miners' Strike of 1984–85, which we give here in our own words, although it is still very current with varying details; our immediate source is the Facebook group '30th anniversary of the miners strike'. The South Yorkshire coalfield was the heartland of the National Union of Mineworkers; the NUM headquarters were at Sheffield, and the planned closure of the colliery at Cortonwood was the final spark that ignited the year-long dispute.

A number of pits are mentioned as places where the snowman incident took place. We have read of Grimethorpe and Kiveton on social media. But in all the versions we have heard, the police officer involved is named as Nesbitt, and is portrayed as a prominent figure in the policing of the strike, widely despised by many miners. Conflict between police and mining communities was pervasive and acrimonious throughout the strike, and there are many stories of confrontations between them.

After the mass pickets at Orgreave and elsewhere, when hundreds of strikers and police had engaged in pitched and running battles, a law was passed banning flying pickets at the pitheads and stating that there were to be no more than six men on a picket line. In the winter of 1984, there was a chief inspector called Nesbitt who would drive around in a plush, heated Range Rover, checking that there were no more than six on any picket.

The winter was bitterly cold, and the regulation six pickets were usually to be found huddled round a brazier in the snow. Nesbitt pulled up one day at the pithead at a certain colliery, in his Range Rover, to find that the six pickets had made themselves a snowman. The snowman was wearing a policeman's helmet and a Coal Board hi-viz tabard. A couple of duty constables were keeping an eye on the picket line. Nesbitt hailed them over and asked them what they thought they were doing about the snowman.

'It's an affront to the law,' the chief inspector said. 'I want it taken down.'

The constables remonstrated, and there was an altercation. In the end the chief inspector lost his patience.

'If you two aren't going to take that thing down,' he told them, 'then I am.'

Nesbitt reversed his Range Rover, wheel-spinning and spattering police and pickets with sludge. The six pickets scattered hurriedly. Nesbitt gunned the engine, and rammed the snowman. The Range Rover ploughed into the seventh picket and the inoffensive-looking snowman vanished into the annals of labour history in a fountain of snow.

But the snowman did good work for his comrades that day. He had been built around a reinforced concrete bollard. The chief inspector's luxurious Range Rover was towed away, a complete write-off.

THE LAMB IN THE CRIB

Paul Davenport reports this story from memory, as it was told him by friends and acquaintances over the years on the local music and dance scene. He would be asking about local songs. On more than one occasion the response would go more or less as follows. We cannot credit the original storytellers, but we quote Paul's account word for word. 'On one occasion,' he writes, 'we were told that Matt lived at Greasborough, and on the other that he lived in Wentworth.'

'He should ask old Matt shouldn't he?'

'Aye, old Matt'd know some old songs.'

'Old Matt knows a lot of stuff, I reckon.'

'Aye [*laughs*] – remember when he nicked that lamb?'

'Oh aye [*laughs*], lucky he wasn't banged up for that! Mind you, his missus was a sharp one.'

'That she was. Sharp, no mistake.'

'Ye see [*turning to Paul*], he'd got this lamb off a farmer's field and took it home ... police got tipped off, though, and went after him. When they got into t house, there was no lamb.'

'Aye, his missus had wrapped it in a sheet and put it in t crib like a babby.'

'Course, police didn't spot it, so went off. Sergeant says to Matt, "I feel sorry for yon babby – he looks just like his dad!"'

As Paul Davenport notes, the tale of a thief who disguises a stolen sheep as a baby is central to the Second Shepherd's Play *of the Wakefield Mystery Cycle, which was first written down in the mid-fifteenth century.*

Medieval mystery plays were based on religious and biblical stories, and they were performed by local community groups, in streets, on carts and other public places, or in bespoke private performances. The Second Shepherd's Play *is a Nativity play for adults, from the perspective of the shepherds of Luke's Gospel. One of their sheep is stolen by the local thief, Mak, and hidden by his wife in a crib, under a blanket. When the shepherds arrive, looking for their sheep, she tries to claim that she has just given birth. This ruse fails when the suspicious shepherds lift the new baby's blanket, asking to kiss it ('Give me leave him to kiss, and lift up the clout. What the devil is this? He has a long snout! ... He is like to our sheep!'). The shepherds then give Mak a good beating, and leave. Only at that point do they encounter an angel tells them to go to Bethlehem. Performance of the cycles was suppressed by the Protestant authorities in 1576.*

The same plot also crops up in an unrelated Jewish folk tale, and elsewhere, which suggests that it was not a new story when the medieval play was composed. It has been suggested that the play incorporates traditional jokes and horseplay indulged over years of repeated rehearsal and performance of the play within communities. This seems plausible to us.

9

'TOMORROW FOR THEE': SOUTH YORKSHIRE DEATH

THE GHOST ARMY OF ROCHE ABBEY

About this same time, in the month of May, near an abbacy called Roche, in the northern part of England, there appeared bands of well-armed knights, riding on valuable horses, with standards and shields, coats of mail and helmets, and decorated with other military equipments; they issued from the earth, as it appeared, and disappeared again into the earth. This vision lasted for several days, and attracted the eyes of those who beheld it, as if by fascination; they rode in arrayed troops, and sometimes engaged in conflict, sometimes as if at a tournament, they shivered their spears into small fragments with a crash; the inhabitants saw them, but more from a distance than near them, for they never remembered to have seen such a fight before, and many said that the occurrence was not without its presage.

This account is given for the year 1236 by the medieval chronicler-monk Matthew Paris (in Bohn's translation, as cited by Aveling (1870)).

Many hauntings have been reported at Roche Abbey over the years. A Grey Lady is said to be visible in the Abbey House (built after the Dissolution), standing at one of the windows and staring out on to the grounds. A wailing child can be heard in one of the upper rooms. A maid is glimpsed disappearing up a flight of stairs. A figure in white has been seen crossing the grass behind the gate-house. Most of these reports and experiences have little in the way of story to go with them, but it is said that an unmarried maidservant at the Abbey House killed her own newborn baby before hanging herself in the attic.

Towards the far end of the abbey itself, there lies a small stone coffin without a lid. One who stares long enough at the head of the coffin is said to see a face.

Why the coffin was never used remains a mystery.

THE ABBOT MONK OF CONISBROUGH

On the night before today
In castel built of Conisbro stone
Myne eyes have seen Phantom
Of Abbot Monk alowne
In the castel with a candel lyt
He was only in castel chapel
Wore he did not syt
Ome at Mecesboro

Bettey my wife I towld of the Phantom and she spowk. No mower must you spake now of them fantommy fowk.

I was cauld, caulder than fust man that deed, and scayed, but I be not scayed or could no mower.

O pray for the curst Cunisbro Abbott Monk that wrought this hour to me! May the Lord take pity on hym and take me wen I dee.

This verse, attributed to Richard Glassby and dated 7 July 1778, is quoted by (among others) Marion Broadhurst in a 1997 letter, citing the Lyonnell Copley Chronicles.

Doncaster Free Press 27-3-1997 (RALS).

HICKLETON CHURCH

Several stories are told to account for the three human skulls set in an alcove in the lychgate of St Wilfrid's church at Hickleton. They are said to have belonged to sheep-thieves; local highwaymen; wayward servant girls; or others hanged for various misdemeanours, and then decapitated as a warning to others. The alcove bears the words:

Today for me. Tomorrow for thee.

Nowadays the legend is also given in Latin – *Hodie mihi cras tibi.*

St Wilfrid's church dates to the twelfth century. There has been a place of worship on the site since Saxon times. The current installation of skulls is a recent restoration, replacing an older one, which bore the inscription in English only.

   The original skulls are believed to have been in place at least since the late 1800s. In these years the church was extensively restored, largely at the expense of the Woods, a local landowning family who were leading lights of the Anglo-Catholic revival; St Wilfrid's retains a proudly Anglo-Catholic tradition in its worship. Charles Wood, who became head of the family in 1885, was an avid reader and collector of ghost stories, so installing the skulls as a decoration would accord well with his taste for the gothic and macabre. The idea that they were executed criminals has persisted, and it is not wholly implausible. In the 1880s, the famous public gibbeting of the high-wayman Spence Broughton on Attercliffe Common was still well within living memory. In 2014, Peter Loades of Wombwell reported that the Great North Road, which now runs east of Hickleton, used to run more or less right past St Wilfrid's, by Hickleton Hall (now a Sue Ryder home), and that the skulls were those of highway-men, gibbeted by the roadside as a deterrent in exactly this manner. Terence Whitaker, a writer on the supernatural, reports having seen a ghostly highwayman at Hickleton in 1953. Hangman's Stone Lane (a source of legend in its own right, as we have seen, above) runs nearby, towards the A1.

The skulls, St Wilfrid's church, Hickleton

Hodie mihi cras tibi, *the Latin version of the phrase, is mentioned by Joseph Kenworthy, in a private letter to Addy, as part of the epitaph for one Francis Morton in Silkstone church.*

South Yorkshire Times 4-11-1994 (RALS); Joseph Kenworthy, private correspondence to S.O. Addy (Sheffield Archives and Local Studies Addy Collection 64-377).

JASPER THE WHISTLER

Despite its name, the Saxon Hotel at Kiveton Park is a new building, dating from around 1960. Nevertheless, it is reputedly haunted by a mischievous presence that moves furniture, knocks ornaments off shelves (in full view of onlookers), and generates strange noises – bumps, bangs and (particularly in the cellar) whistles and disembodied footsteps. The spirit is known as 'Jasper', said to have been a monk who lived in the nearby chantry chapel. Following his death (by murder), he haunted a nearby house, before moving into the Saxon.

Although in some ways disconcerting (particularly to family dogs), Jasper was regarded as a 'very friendly ghost', and in 1972 the landlord of the Saxon refused permission to a group of psychic investigators to inquire further. He told journalists: 'Jasper doesn't upset anybody, so I thought the best thing we can do is not disturb him. There's no point having him upset.' About a decade later, in T.W. Whittaker's *Yorkshire Ghosts and Legends*, the Saxon inn ghost appeared as 'The Whistler', said to haunt the cellar particularly, and, as his name implies, to signal his presence by whistling. The details of the haunting were different, but they were still being explained with reference to the ghost of the murdered monk.

Rotherham Advertiser 23-6-1972; *Worksop Guardian*
11-7-1987 (RALS); Whittaker 1983: 98-9.

THE THIEVING MILKMAID

Among the numerous gargoyles on Aston church is one with a story attached. The figure – now much eroded – shows a naked woman, holding a creamer and a milk pail, suspended upside down in the clutches of the Devil. This is said to represent a maid who, in about 1350:

... lived at the Hall just beyond the churchyard wall. The squire allowed her a certain quantity of milk daily to distribute to the poor of the village, but the maid took a part of this and diluted it with water up to the original quantity, which she devoted to the donor's purpose, selling the rest for her own profit. When found out she was anathema, and this was part of her punishment – to hang in effigy forever, head downwards, nude to all the winds that blow, in the close clasp of the Prince of Darkness, while a subordinate imp heaps indignity on her.

The remains of the thieving maid gargoyle at All Saints' church, Aston

Featuring in the humiliating gargoyle seems to be the limit of the maid's punishment, rather than the Devil literally carrying her off. But in either case it seems to be the carving that inspired the story, and not the other way about – a common possibility.

Rotherham Advertiser 14-9-1935.

THORPE HESLEY BOGGART

Nowadays the famous Thorpe Hesley Boggart is sometimes said to be the ghost of Thomas Wentworth, a Royalist politician from the local landowning family, who was executed in 1641 following (allegedly) his arrest under an oak tree in Tankersley Park. His ghost, said the Rotherham Advertiser *in 1943, walks down 'Haigh Lane' (Hague Lane?) from Wentworth Woodhouse with its head under its arm.*

However, John Chessman (n.d.: 14) mentions a Sheffield newspaper cutting from 1875 in which the Thorpe Hesley Boggart is explained either as the spirit of a local hanged man, or as a hoax perpetrated by body-snatchers to scare potential witnesses away from graveyards. In any case, the boggart's restless to-ing and fro-ing gave rise to a local proverb: a restless person (or thing) could be said to 'come and go like the Thorpe Hesley Boggart'.

Chessman also tells a story of a prank played on the basis of the legend, which we give here in his words.

The story is told of a number of miners in the early part of this [i.e. the twentieth] century arranging to play a joke on one of their colleagues from Scholes.

Knowing he had to travel via the 'shortlands', the churchyard and the 'crofts' on the way to the pit, they planned that one of their number would act as a ghost.

Early one cold dark winter morning he waited beside an open grave with a white sheet over him.

As the man from Scholes drew near he began to walk round the grave chanting,

Hague Lane, looking towards Thorpe Hesley

'I can't get in, I can't get in.'

The Scholes man, a little surprised and afraid at first, soon realised it was a joke, so he went up to the 'ghost' and sarcastically remarked, 'All rate, owd chap, if that's ha tha feels, ha'll help thi.' Forthwith he pushed him into the grave and went on his way to work with a feeling of something well done.

Rotherham Advertiser 24-12-1942, 9-1-1943, 22-10-1982 (RALS); *Rotherham Star* 19-10-1982 (RALS).

THE LUDWELL WIFE

'At the corner of the road to Marr, on the Barnbrough to Doncaster high road,' writes the *Sheffield Miscellany*, 'are the three cottages called Ludwell Houses.' The cottages were made up from a derelict farmhouse in the 1860s. Since the later 1700s, seemingly, this farmhouse had been haunted by a headless ghost known as the Ludwell Wife. In the course of the 1860s renovation, a headless skeleton was indeed found buried in the garden; it was reinterred in consecrated ground, but, some years later, a wild cherry tree in the same garden was torn up by the roots by a strong wind, and a skull was uncovered, lying among the roots. The reburial seems to have brought peace to the unquiet spirit and she has ceased to walk.

Sheffield Miscellany: 42 (Sheffield Archives and Local Studies).

THE GREY LADY OF AUCKLEY

'The name of the Grey Lady is unknown, but it's believed that she was the youngest daughter of a village man who never let her marry. As a result, the lonely girl took solace in other people's happiness and, after her death, she made appearances at weddings and christenings for more than three hundred years, usually as a grey apparition at the back of the room. As she was believed to pose no threat, the villagers soon adopted her, and it became customary on feast days to set a place for her at the table. A special toast was made for her:

> We wish thee joy on this our celebration.
> Come sit thee down and take a glass of wine.
> And if you sup in our felicitation.
> The hour is blest as blessed you may be.

Auckley, east of Doncaster, has a number of ghosts, including several at the Eagle and Child. The name of this inn (and other inns with the same name) famously references the legend of Oskell of Lathom – but, since Lathom Park is in Lancashire, we naturally scorn to include it in a book about Yorkshire. You'll just have to look it up.

'The Grey Lady of Auckley', www.bbc.co.uk/southyorkshire/ sense_of_place/ghost_stories/grey_lady.shtml, accessed 4-1-2015.

Aston: the Rectory Ghosts

Three bodies are supposed to be buried in the rectory garden at Aston. One is that of a highwayman who broke into a house when the man of the house was at market. The intruder demanded food and drink from the wife and her servant. Shrewdly, the women fed him so much, and gave him so much ale, that he grew drowsy, fell asleep in a chair and began to snore. The servant girl then emptied a boiling kettle into his open mouth and killed him outright.

The other two bodies are those of a man and his married lover; in a jealous fit he murdered her, and then committed suicide.

The Rectory (now High Trees), All Saints' church, Aston

A tangle of rumours relating to violent death and hauntings cling to the former Aston Rectory – nowadays, High Trees, opposite the church on Church Lane. Local historian Charles Colley Bailey, author of a History of Aston, *reported the above story to the* Rotherham Advertiser *in 1954; the story of the highwayman and the kettle is widespread, and Katharine Briggs records a similar tale in East Anglia in the 1930s.* The Star, *meanwhile, in 1959 reported first-hand experiences of strange goings-on at the rectory – footsteps, and sightings of the figure of a shadowy Grey Lady, explained by rumours that, 'the body of the rector's young wife was found murdered in a windowless room leading off the back stairs … the rector's own butler was caught and executed for the crime.'*

In this second report, there is no outright mention of a lover's murderous jealousy, but the mention of a butler and a rector's wife might suggest it – and if the priest's wife really was murdered by her own servant-lover, this may suggest why she might be buried discreetly in the rectory grounds. But in 1991 Charles Colley Bailey wrote again to the Advertiser, *explicitly to squash this conclusion. He explained that the murdered woman (whose ghost was indeed doing the haunting) was Dorothy, a servant. He added that Dorothy appears when strife is pending in the house, and that the house had been exorcised.*

The Star *2-6-1959 (RALS);* Rotherham Advertiser
22-7-1988, 8-11-1991 (RALS); Cf. 'The Brave Maid-
Servant,' Briggs 1991 (1970) Part B, Vol. 4: 171.

SHEFFIELD: THE CAMPO LANE BARGUEST

Joseph Woolhouse of Sheffield, writing perhaps as early as the 1830s, described a large house in Smith Street (now part of Leopold Street) where his aunt once lived. 'I have heard her and the rest of the family say that they have heard dreadful noises in the street at midnight many a time,' he wrote, before going on to tell the following extraordinary story, of a man cured of lameness by running from a barguest (demon). We give Woolhouse's account word for word.

My Grandfather … lived at Green Lane and kept a public house …

One of his men was lame and compell'd to have Crutches to assist him to travel for a number of Years …

This person was out late one evening and had to come on Campo Lane, he saw (or fancied he saw) the Bargast (as it has been frequently called) coming towards him on Campo Lane. At that time the Paradise Square was a field with a Stile at the top to go over. When he first saw this goblin he thought within himself, 'If I can but get over this stile into the field I can go down the hill merrily.' … He managed it over this Stile, but the fiend gained ground on him. Faster he went and faster it followed, he ran with his Crutches till his fears came thicker and faster, and this demon still getting nearer, when, being about the middle of this field (the Square) seeing this goblin close at his heels, he there dropt his Crutches and away went he without them, and never stopt or look'd behind him until he got home (he lived in Gregory Row, a very narrow thoroughfare out of West Bar Green …).

The wife had the door made, but him being in such a fright had not patience to wait until she opened the door but burst it open. He told the wife what was at the door, but she was the worse frightened at him coming without his Crutches than at the Bargast. However, they were a little reconciled and went to bed. He could not rest from fright, and got up at daylight the next morning to go in quest of his Crutches; he found them in exactly the same place where he dropt them. He went to his work the next morning and his Shopmen was nearly as frightened to see him come trotting to the shop without his crutches as he was when he saw the Bargast. However, he was so overjoyed that he gave his Shopmen a treat of some ale, and they spent the day Cheerfully; and he for his own part never used Crutches again while he lived, and he lived a many years after this.

Joseph Woolhouse was born in 1778. He worked, says Henry Richardson, as a cutler, after obtaining his freedom to practise in 1801. He took up his post as a 'time-keeper at Sheaf Works' in 1833. He wrote prolifically in his spare time, his most productive years falling between 1821 and 1842. He would lend his manuscripts out for a small fee, and read them aloud in pubs. Richardson acquired Woolhouse's manuscripts around 1900. He published them, writing a foreword to the Description *(Woolhouse n.d.) in 1926.*

If Woolhouse's grandfather was keeping an inn when this story took place, then it would seem to place the story a little before the 1730s, when the construction of Paradise Square began, over the field called Hick's Stile. Campo Lane might have been slightly off the disabled man's usual beat; his home off West Bar Green, and his workplace on Green Lane, would have been at the foot of the hill, close to the River Don at Kelham Island. This barguest is not the only urban demon in Sheffield, or the most recent; the so-called Hillsborough Padfoot was encountered by a local police officer, one snowy night in the late 1960s.

Old Moult

A ghost known as Old Moult (Moulte or Moat) was said to haunt Morthen Road in Wickersley, and stories were told of him relating to Wickersley Grange, on Morthen Road. W. Sorby Briggs, rector of Wickersley, reported them (1954: 129–33). We begin our account of Old Moult with the rector's own words:

I have never seen this ghost, but some of the older residents say they have. The name is a corruption of Moult, which was the surname of a gentleman who lived at the Grange in the eighteenth century. He is supposed to ride near the Grange and on Morthen Road at about midnight in bad weather on winter's nights. January is supposed to be a favoured time of the year for his rides.

Britain seemed to be on the brink of revolution in the later 1700s: the global revolution that had recently triumphed in Britain's American colonies, and in the ancient kingdom of France, seemed to be spreading everywhere. Sheffield in these years was a rowdy, rebellious boom town: not a place for the faint-hearted, but certainly a place where hard work, hard money and hard drink were plentiful. People flocked in their thousands to work and play as hard as they could. They found a town that had been proudly self-reliant for centuries, and neither natives nor newcomers seemed to have much truck with courts or kings. Such was the fear of an uprising that a troop of redcoats had been stationed permanently in the city. This treatment was like a red rag to a bull: the respectable-sounding Sheffield Contitutional Information Society was really a movement agitating for parliamentary reform, and Sheffield's narrow streets were the scenes of nightly unrest in the same cause.

Robert Wilde Moult was a shy man who had the misfortune to be seeking a quiet life in these unquiet times. He dwelt alone in Wickersley Grange, when it was still a 'long, one-storey building with peaked gables and a thatched roof', rattling around in the big old house with only his own wandering thoughts for company. His father Samuel had been a Presbyterian minister, and his mother, Bridget Wylde, belonged to a prominent landowning local family. A 'learned eccentric', Moult had spent his life amassing a huge archive of materials relating to the history and heritage of Wickersley. The Grange was a treasure trove of medieval charters and documents.

Wickersley Grange

One night in 1794, Moult was woken by a furious battering at his door. It was the redcoats, who tramped into the Grange and immediately began turning it upside down, in search of papers or other evidence that would prove Moult to be a French spy. One of the neighbours had tipped them off: Old Moult, with his endless preoccupation with mysterious writings, seemed to be up to no good, and the Grange – so the troops were given to understand – harboured 'a person then obnoxious to the Government'. They ransacked the Grange without turning up anything suspicious at all, and, duty done, the troops left Old Moult alone amid the wreckage of his home. The eccentric old man had taken a terrible fright, and the next morning, apparently in simple, blind terror, he burned his entire archive in a brazier in the garden of the Grange. Charters and parchments went up in the steady drift of smoke, until nothing was left but the title deeds of Moult's own estates. And nothing more remains of Moult's archive to this day.

Moult died in 1810, aged 63: one among many little-remembered victims of a little-remembered campaign of terror by a British Government against its own citizens.

Some say that Moult bequeathed the Grange to a nephew, or to other young relatives. He left the house on condition that it remained unaltered. But no sooner was the old man in his grave, and the title deeds transferred, than the new owner (or owners) embarked on renovating the roof.

And there, in the rafters, they discovered a hoard of gold coins.

There were those who said that Old Moult could not rest quiet in his grave following this affront. After the alterations to the house, he was often seen riding his favourite white pony, or walking headless on the precincts of Wickersley Grange, on New Year's Eve or other winter nights. He is also reported to have pulled bedclothes off sleeping servants. In 1896, Harold Wild wrote that, 'many of the villagers hardly care to cross the Grange paddock after nightfall, so great is their dread of 'owd Mote'.' And one January evening, around 1948, W. Sorby Briggs commented on the wintry weather to an old lady of the parish, who replied: 'Yes, just the sort of night for Old Moat to ride in.' Briggs was writing in the 1950s as if his parishioners were still in the habit of taking the ghost at least half-seriously.

It is not hard to see how a spirit such as Moult's might have rested uneasy, even in the grave, once the sanctity of his beloved Grange was violated a second time after his death, as it had been once already in his life – and by his own trusted heirs, to boot. Be that as it may, it seems not altogether unfitting that rumours of Moult's restless spirit are among the few echoes that have come down to the present day of the early and medieval history of Wickersley – the subject which Moult made his life's work, and which was lost forever on the day he destroyed it.

Rotherham Advertiser 26-5-1934, 14-11-1959, 12-12-1986 (RALS); *Morning Telegraph* 26-1-1972 (RALS).

Firbeck Ghosts

Following the tragic death of Catherine West, Firbeck Hall changed hands several times over the centuries, before briefly flourishing as a well-connected country club in the 1930s. It then served as an infirmary for wounded airmen and other military personnel, and then a convalescent home for miners. The hall has stood empty since 1990. The yew trees of Dark Walk have now been felled. Firbeck Hall has become a derelict hang-out for gangs of youths, and its future is uncertain. It remains – as one of us (DB) can confirm from first-hand experience – 'the perfect place to discover that you're not as sceptical as you thought you were.' Below is our retelling of just two of the many stories of strange goings-on at the hall and its environs.

ORD HAMILTON'S STORY

In the 1930s, Firbeck Hall was bought by a stockbroker, and enjoyed a brief heyday as a country club and fashionable resort for the elite. The nearby airfield was well suited to accommodate private aeroplanes. Mr Ord Hamilton, the London bandleader, stayed there in 1935.

After he arrived, he was woken by a bell ringing for several minutes together, between around midnight and two, every night without fail. He mentioned this inconvenience to the staff, only to be told that residents and staff had often likewise been awakened by the tolling of a distant bell, and the source of the sound was unknown and mysterious. Mr Ord Hamilton decided to inquire further.

He discovered something very odd.

There were two bells: one on the roof and one on the back wall outside. The wire pulleys had been removed from both bells, and both were rusted and stiff from disuse and neglect. No amount of weather could have created the sound that the residents had described.

What Ord Hamilton made of the bells we can only speculate, but the following night at two o'clock in the morning, he received a knock at his door. He opened the door to confront an empty corridor, so he closed the door again, at which point all the lights went out.

Then, as he stood in the doorway, plunged into sudden and total darkness, from down the corridor there came a harrowing, high-pitched scream.

Ord Hamilton dared not investigate, but shut himself in his room and waited for morning.

When he asked the staff in the morning what it all might mean, then for the first time he was told the story of the Green Lady of Firbeck Hall. The Green Lady, they said, had been restless lately; a bellboy had rushed into the staff dining room during supper, terrified of the woman in green he had just seen on an upstairs corridor; and a porter had seen her from the window of his lodge by the gate.

ANNIE'S GHOST

Opposite St Martin's church in Firbeck, just to the right of Kidd Lane, lies the entrance to the Park Hill Estate. In the mid-nineteenth century, the estate house known as Haven Lodge was occupied by the Hansons and their two teenage daughters.

One day, Annie Hanson went missing. Months passed by with no clue as to the girl's welfare or whereabouts, and the Hanson family were distraught.

In fact she had fallen pregnant by a man who was staying at Firbeck Hall. In those days, if the news had got out, the whole family would have been evicted. The young girl thought she couldn't have lived with herself if that happened, and she had wandered over to the old Mill Dam and thrown herself in.

One dark night, the girl's uncle, who worked on the estate, was on his way home from the nearby village of Letwell. He had just reached the end of the two adjacent fields along the road when he caught sight of a scantily clad young girl, standing in the cold, in a place where not even fog can settle comfortably.

As he watched, she began to walk over the bridge that separates Firbeck from the countryside, when he caught a glimpse of her face. It was enough of a glimpse for him to recognise his niece, Annie Hanson. He called out to her in relief. But she didn't answer or turn; she only walked along the path to the old Mill Dam. He followed her the entire way behind the estate, only to watch as she disappeared.

The man told his brother what he had seen, and it was the girl's father who then discovered the body of his niece in the old Mill Dam.

Ever since then, there have been many sightings of a young girl at the bottom of Kidd Lane on the bridge, by people unaware of this legend. And Annie's ghost remains in limbo, oblivious that her family would live on at Haven Lodge for many years to come.

Rotherham Advertiser 25-2-2005 (RALS).

MARY ON THE BLACK PIG

In 1981, the cleaner at the Ship mentioned her grandfather's reports of 'having seen ghosts on the canal bank when he was a young man'. The area had a reputation for more than one haunting. In 1994 the *Rotherham Star* reported on the ghost of Mary, said to have been

The Ship Inn, Swinton, with the railway and canal

drowned in the river at Swinton by her drunken farmer husband after she slaughtered his prize pig. Mary, said the report, could still be met with, riding a spectral black pig along the riverside.

South Yorkshire Times 2-1-1981 (RALS); *Rotherham Advertiser* 16-1-1981 (RALS); *Rotherham Star* 8-9-1994 (RALS); *South Yorkshire Times* 4-11-1994 (RALS).

CORTONWOOD PIT

Pit disasters were numerous and terrible throughout the history of South Yorkshire's coalfields. Among the more famous examples was the Huskar Pit flood disaster of 1838, near Silkstone Common, where twenty-six children died. As in the developing world today, mine owners held their workers' lives cheap. In mining – as in many professions involving serious and unpredictable risk – portents and premonitions were, and are, often taken seriously. Through mutual friends, near Thurnscoe, we heard of a miner whose wife's way of letting him know of a premonition of danger was to pointedly fail to get round to making up his lunch in time for him to go on shift. Eventually he would take the hint and not go on shift. The point would be made without ever being mentioned.

Cortonwood, sunk in 1873 to the Barnsley seam, was the colliery that took the first industrial action in the 1984–85 Miners' Strike. It was also the site of an underground fire in 1931. The following account is taken from contemporary newspaper reports, relating to one of the casualties, William Landles.

Landles, who is thirty-one years old, was only married a few years ago. His wife had asked him never to work on night shifts. She thought that if he did he would be brought home – a phrase that has a tragic meaning in colliery districts.

On Thursday night he seemed unwell, his usual cheerfulness having given way to gloom. He decided that, as Christmas was approaching, he would work on the Thursday night shift. His wife begged him not to, but he went. Her premonition was only too terribly fulfilled.

Sheffield Daily Telegraph 10-12-1932 (RALS).

THE GHOST OF WATH MAIN

In 1975 The Star *reported the testimony of a twenty-one-year-old pit electrician at Wath Main Colliery. Opinion was divided among the men as to whether the causes were natural or supernatural.*

There were six of us working near the coalface when it happened. It really scared everyone. I certainly do not want to go there again on my own for a long time. We saw a very bright pit helmet light in the distance walking towards us. We were moving supplies at the time so we waited for him to get to us for safety reasons. But when the light got near to us it just disappeared. We walked down the roadway, but there was no one there. It was just as though it had disappeared through the sides of the tunnel. Two men at the other end of the roadway also saw the light. It was impossible for anyone to be playing a trick because they would have had to pass us. But like everyone else I really didn't believe it [reports of previous sightings], but now I think we have seen something unnatural. A man collapsed and died in this part of the pit two years ago.

The Star 8-11-1975 (RALS); *South Yorkshire Times* 11-11-1975 (RALS); *Morning Telegraph* 10-11-1976 (RALS).

A Bier of Stones

In 1981, a group of schoolgirls from Wales Comprehensive School, aged 14–15, sat in Wales parish church bell tower for forty-eight hours as a charity fundraising stunt. The stunt was considered particularly challenging because the tower was said to be 'haunted by a fifteenth-century corpse' which 'disappeared from its coffin on the way from the nearby village of Thorpe Salvin to Wales church. When opened the coffin was full of stones.'

The girls' resolve was not, in the end, tested by an actual confrontation with the ghost, although, as the *Sheffield Star* reported, 'the timbers of the church creaked ominously'.

Other legends hint at the meaning of this odd story – in similar Irish legends the dead person has often been stolen, sometimes by fairies, and the stones substituted, as ballast, to conceal the theft.

Sheffield Star 21-12-1981 (RALS).

Born Again, Never to Die

The South Yorkshire Times *reported that a child's voice had appeared mysteriously on a cassette tape recording at Kilnhurst, speaking the following words:*

Born again never to die
Born again into your family,
I'm born again, born again.

South Yorkshire Times 17-10-1986, 3-7-1987 (RALS).

THE THREE SISTERS

The high-rise tower blocks at Herdings Park, Sheffield, are now only two in number, but they are still known as the Three Sisters. A number of stories exist to account for this name. Dane Holt, of Chesterfield, told us around 2012 that the blocks were named after three unmarried sisters who lived there – one was murdered by the other two, who were jealous of her forthcoming marriage. A variant or similar story was described by an anonymous poster to the Sheffield History Forum in 2003:

The Three Sisters, Herdings Park

There were three tower blocks at Herdings (there's now only two), and it's said that three sisters, triplets, lived in the flats – one in each, at the top. On the same evening, they were murdered and their bodies placed in a bag and dragged down the stairs, from the twelfth floor to the bottom. They supposedly haunt the remaining two blocks, and that one night each year bloodstains appear on the stairs of each block.

'Ever heard of Springheel Jack?' Post to discussion board by 'DaBouncer',
www.sheffieldforum.co.uk/archive/index.php/t-303372.html,
accessed 7-9-2013. Quoted word for word.

My tale's ended,
T door-sneck's bended;
I went into t garden
To get a bit o thyme;
I've telled my tale,
Thee tell thine.

Addy 1895.

SELECTED
REFERENCES

Anon., 'The Hangman's Stone', *Notes and Queries 2*, Vol. 1
(September 1899), p. 92

Addy, Sidney Oldall, *Household Tales with other Traditional Remains
Collected in the Counties of York, Lincoln, Derby and Nottingham*
(London: David Nutt; Sheffield: Pawson and Brailsford, 1895)

Armitage, Ella S., *A Key to English Antiquities with Special
Reference to the Sheffield and Rotherham District* (Sheffield: Wm.
Townsend, 1897)

Armstrong, Ted, 'The Cat and Man Legend of Barnburgh',
Northern Earth Mysteries, Vol. 10 (April 1980)

Atkins, J., *Myths and Legends of Stanyton & Roundabout* (1983)

Aveling, James H., *The History of Roche Abbey, from its Foundation
to its Dissolution* (London and Worksop: John Russell Smith
and Robert White, 1870)

Barnburgh St Peter's Mothers' Union, *The Legend of the Cat and
Man* (1993)

Bell, Sean, and Glyn Davie, '5–7 Station Road, Conisbrough,
South Yorkshire', Archaeological Desk-Based Assessment.
Report 1180.1(1). ARCUS 2008. (http://archaeologydataser-
vice.ac.uk/catalogue/adsdata/arch-908-1/dissemination/pdf/
arcus2-38634_1.pdf, accessed 30-10-2012)

Bennett, Gillian, *Traditions of Belief: Women and the Supernatural*
(London: Penguin, 1987)

Bett, Henry, *English Legends* (London: Batsford, 1950)

Biggs, Paul, and Sandra Biggs, *Discovery Walks in Derbyshire* (Wilmslow: Sigma Press, 1997)

Briggs, Katharine M., *A Dictionary of British Folk-Tales in the English Language, Incorporating the F.J. Norton Collection,* parts A (Vols 1–2) and B (Vols 3–4) (London and New York: Routledge, 1991 (1970))

Briggs, W. Sorby, *Wickersley: The Story of a Village* (1954)

Camden, William, *Britannia, or a Chorographical Description of GREAT BRITAIN and IRELAND, Together with the Adjacent Islands,* tr. and ed. by Edmund Gibson (University of Adelaide, 1722) (http://ebooks.adelaide.edu.au/c/camden/william/britannia-gibson-1722/)

Chessman, John Robert, *Thorpe Hesley: Its Past, Its Places, Its People* (n.d.)

Child, Francis James (ed.) *The English and Scottish Popular Ballads,* 5 vols (New York: Dover Publications Inc., 1965 (1882–98))

Clarke, David, and Rob Wilson, *Strange Sheffield: Legends, Folklore and Mysteries of Hallamshire* (High Wycombe: ASSAP, 1987)

Dallas, F.H., *The Legends of Thorne,* Occasional Paper, No. 18 (Thorne Local History Society, 1995)

Davenport, Paul, *Total Eclipse: The Story of the Blind Musicians of Sheffield 1790–1850* (2011) (www.hallamtrads.co.uk)

Deacon, George, *John Clare and the Folk Tradition* (London: Francis Boutle, 2002 (1983))

Eastwood, T.S.B., *Ivanhoe-Land: Being Notes on Men and Books Connected with the Town and Neighbourhood of Rotherham* (Rotherham: Gilling, 1865)

Ewen, C. l'Estrange, *Witchcraft and Demonianism* (Muller, 1933)

Firth, Fiona, 'Cataclysmic!' *The Star* 25-1-2003.

Geoffrey of Monmouth, *The History of the Kings of Britain,* tr. Lewis Thorpe (Harmondsworth: Penguin, 1986 (1966))

Green, Barbara, *The Outlaw Robin Hood: His Yorkshire Legend* (Huddersfield: Kirkless Cultural Services, 1991)

Henderson, William, *Folk Lore of the Northern Counties of England and the Borders* (East Ardsley: EP Publishing, 1973 (1866))

Ingledew, J. Davison, *The Ballads and Songs of Yorkshire*, transcribed from *Private Manuscripts, Rare Broadsides, and Scarce Publications, with Notes and a Glossary* (London: Bell and Daldy, 1860)

Kitchen, Fred, *Brother to the Ox: An Autobiography of an Agricultural Labourer* (Caliban Books, 1981 (1939))

Kristen, Clive, *Local Ghost Trails* (Wharncliffe Books, 1998)

Langdale, Thomas, *Topographical Dictionary of Yorkshire* (1822) (https://play.google.com/books/reader?id=HLAKAAAAYAAJ& printsec=frontcover&output=reader&authuser=0&hl=en&pg= GBS.PR1, accessed 29-12-2012)

Mather, Joseph, *The Songs of Joseph Mather: to which are added a memoir of Mather, and miscellaneous songs relating to Sheffield. With introduction and notes by John Wilson* (Sheffield: Pawson and Brailsford, 1862)

McCormick, Charlie T. and Kim Magoun, Jr., F.P., Review of J.H. Cockburn, 'The Battle of Brunanburh and its Period elucidated by Place-Names', *Speculum 8* (1933), pp. 85–87.

McCormick, Charlie T. and Kennedy White (eds), *Folklore: An Encyclopedia of Beliefs, Customs, Tales, Music, and Art* (Santa Barbara, ABC-CLIO, 2011)

Mitchell, W.R., *The Haunts of Robin Hood* (Clapham: Dalesman, 1970)

Naylor, John Anderton, and Robert Anderton Naylor, *From John O'Groats to Land's End, Or 1372 Miles on Foot: A Book of Days and Chronicle of Adventures by Two Pedestrians on Tour* (London: Caxton Publishing Company, 1916) (www.gutenberg.org/ebooks/14415, release date 22-12-2004, accessed 30-10-2012)

Off the Cuff, *What Difference Does It Make?* (Dead Records DEAD002, 1987)

Parkinson, Thomas, *Yorkshire Legends and Traditions, as told by her Ancient Chroniclers, Her Poets, and Journalists* (London: Elliott Stock, 1889)

Phinn, Gervase, *Road to the Dales: The Story of a Yorkshire Lad* (London: Penguin, 2010)

Pratt, Charles T., *A History of Cawthorne* (Barnsley: Private Publication, 1882)

de la Pryme, Abraham, *Diary of Abraham de la Pryme*, Vol. 54
    (Surtees Society, 1869)

Randles, Jenny, *Supernatural Pennines* (London: Robert Hale, 2002)

Ray, John, and John Belfour, *A Complete Collection of English
    Proverbs: Also, the most celebrated proverbs of the Scotch, Italian,
    French, Spanish, and Other Languages* (G. Cowie & Co., 1813)

Robins, Philip, and Ray Sickler, *The Story of Todwick as Told by
    Villagers Old and New* (n.d.)

Rooney, Kevin, assisted by Peter Hawkridge, *Rook Town: A History
    of Scholes, Rotherham* (Clifton Local History Group, 2004)

Sanderson, Doug, *A Layman's Look at the History, People and
    Places of Oughtibridge, Worrall, and Wharncliffe Side* (Sheffield:
    ALD Design and Print, 2001 (1999))

Smith, David T., 'The Smiths of Yorkshire and Glen
    Sherr: An Agricultural Family', *Transactions of the Hunter
    Archaeological Society,* VIII (offprint, 1960)

Smith, Roly, *Yorkshire County Memories* (Salisbury: Francis Frith
    Collection, 2003)

Taylor, E. (ed.), *German Popular Stories*, tr. from the *Kinder- und
    Haus-Märchen*, collected by M.M. Grimm from oral tradition
    (London: C. Baldwin, 1823)

Taylor, J. *et al.*, *Unto Brigg Fair: Joseph Taylor and Other
    Traditional Lincolnshire Singers Recorded in 1908 by Percy
    Grainger* (Leader Records LEA4050, 1972)

Tomlinson, John, *Rambles Twenty Miles Round Doncaster*
    (Doncaster: Robert Hartley, 1860) (https://play.google.com/
    store/books/details?id=Ir8HAAAAQAAJ)

Tomlinson, John, *Stories and Sketches Relating to Yorkshire*
    (London: Simpkin, Marshall & Co.; Doncaster:
    R. Hartley, 1868) (https://play.google.com/store/books/
    details?id=HrQHAAAAQAAJ)

Tangherlini, Timothy R., *Interpreting Legend: Danish Storytellers
    and Their Repertoires* (New York and London: Garland, 1994)

Tunney, John, 'Cats and Kings,' *Eastside* (January 1992)

Vickers, J. Edward, *Tales and Legends of Ancient Sheffield*
    (Sheffield: JEV Publications, 1973)

Ward, Clifford, *St Peter's: The Story of a Christian Church* (Barnburgh, n.d.)

Westwood, Jennifer, and Jacqueline Simpson, *The Lore of the Land: A Guide to England's Legends, from Spring-Heeled Jack to the Witches of Warboys* (Harmondsworth: Penguin, 2006 (2005))

Whittaker, T.W., *Yorkshire Ghosts and Legends* (Granada, 1983)

Wilson, C.H., *Wincobank and Blackburn: A History of the Lower Blackburn Valley* (Kimberworth, 1996)

Wilson, Cyril, *Brinsworth and Tinsley: A History of the Area* (Kimberworth, 1994)

Wood, Michael, *In Search of England* (London: Penguin, 1999)

Woolhouse, Joseph, *A DESCRIPTION OF THE TOWN OF SHEFFIELD in my remembrance wrote in the year 1832 at the time the Cholera was raging in Sheffield,* transcribed by Eric Youle (n.d.) (http://youle.info/history/fh_material/sheffield_circa_1800.txt, accessed 4-1-2015)

Society for Storytelling

Since 1993, the Society for Storytelling has championed the art of oral storytelling and the benefits it can provide – such as improving memory more than rote learning, promoting healing by stimulating the release of neuropeptides, or simply great entertainment! Storytellers, enthusiasts and academics support and are supported by this registered charity to ensure the art is nurtured and developed throughout the UK.

Many activities of the Society are available to all, such as locating storytellers on the Society website, taking part in our annual National Storytelling Week at the start of every February, purchasing our quarterly magazine *Storylines*, or attending our Annual Gathering – a chance to revel in engaging performances, inspiring workshops, and the company of like-minded people.

You can also become a member of the Society to support the work we do. In return, you receive free access to *Storylines*, discounted tickets to the Annual Gathering and other story-telling events, the opportunity to join our mentorship scheme for new storytellers, and more. Among our great deals for members is a 30% discount off titles in the *Folk Tales* series from The History Press website.

For more information, including how to join, please visit

www.sfs.org.uk